The Small Business Guide to the Internet

A Practical Approach to Going Online

Richard G. Lewis

Oak Tree Press

Dublin

Oak Tree Press
Merrion Building
Lower Merrion Street
Dublin 2, Ireland
www.oaktreepress.com

A catalogue record of this book is
available from the British Library.

ISBN 1 86076 146 1

Printed in Ireland by
Colour Books Ltd.

ABOUT THE AUTHOR

Richard G. Lewis BA (Hons) MSc is a freelance business consultant specialising in e-commerce and marketing. Richard was educated at the University of Glamorgan where he attained degrees
in both business and computing. He has experience of managing
small businesses in the marketing, retail, leisure and service industries. He is currently designing and building web sites for
various clients in the retail and Internet solutions sectors.

CONTENTS

PART TWO: GOING ONLINE

PART THREE: DOING BUSINESS ON THE INTERNET

DEDICATION

Dedicated to the memory of Bryn Clunn. With special thanks to my parents who supported me without complaint. Thanks also to Martin Baker, a genius and a gentleman.

1

INTRODUCTION

The European Commission has recently acknowledged the importance of e-commerce in the development of future global markets:

> "As the world develops a digital economy, the importance of on-line business will continue to grow" (Stefano Micossi, Director General of Industry (DGIII), 1998).[1]

Experts also recognise that this new Internet-based (online) economy will be driven by entrepreneurs and small businesses rather than the large global corporations dominating the present world economy:

> "Entrepreneurs are seizing the opportunities today's technology offers . . . entrepreneurs are driving e-commerce forward and altering the way society does business" (David Wilkinson, Ernst & Young's National Head of Entrepreneurial Services, 1999).[2]

As a consequence of predictions such as these all small businesses are coming under increasing pressure to take up electronic commerce . . . "or be left behind". However, only specific small businesses are in fact suited to Internet commerce. Millions of pounds are indeed being made by certain Internet-based small businesses, but those that are not suited to Internet commerce are losing money. It is hoped that the analysis and advice in this book will serve as a guide to those small businesses considering trading over the Internet.

The purpose of this book is to help you evaluate whether or not your specific small business can derive competitive advantage from the use of Internet commerce or by establishing an Internet presence. Part 1 evaluates the correct *strategic fit* between small business and the World Wide Web (W3, WWW or Web), to help judge which specific businesses are suited to e-commerce. This section also outlines which Internet-based businesses are already profitable, as well as predicting which businesses may be profitable in the future. To help define and evaluate which businesses do possess the correct strategic fit for e-commerce, Part 1 concludes by looking at actual case studies of small firms that have recently implemented I-solutions, or are considering e-commerce, as part of their business strategy.

Part 2 considers the process of setting up an Internet-based business. It describes the equipment necessary to go on-line, how to access the Internet, the likely start-up costs, how to design your web site and what you should put on it.

Part 3 then offers advice on doing business on-line: reaching potential customers, effective marketing strategies, creating consumer trust, handling electronic payments, doing market research and concludes with a look at issues of security on the Internet.

THE SMALL BUSINESS SECTOR

This business sector plays an essential part in job creation and in the development of innovations (not least of all, in the computer industry) throughout the European economy. However, currently, only about 30 per cent of owner-manager firms in Europe trade over the Internet. This figure is bolstered mainly by the Scandinavian countries who are more enthusiastic about e-commerce, and telecommunications in general, than the rest of Europe. For example, 58 per cent of Swedish companies already have commercial web sites.

According to researcher IDC, global e-commerce will be worth £563 billion by 2003.[3] Experts predict that European businesses will generate £156 billion in e-commerce over the next three years, mostly benefiting small firms due to its low costs and huge consumer audience. Yet it is this very business sector that is the least well informed regarding Internet commerce. The present UK government has acknowledged the importance of small business as the prime economic driver of the future:

> "This government is committed to the creation of an enterprise economy. Small companies are the lifeblood of such an economy and it is obvious that if we are to drive forward the competitiveness of British industry we must have a dynamic and visionary small business sector. . . . And as we move towards the 21st century it is vital that small firms in particular exploit the advantages of information technology" (Barbara Roche, UK Minister for Small Business, 1998).[4]

In May 1999, at the Dublin conference of the International Commerce Exchange (ICX), the Irish government revealed its plans to develop Ireland as a global centre for e-commerce. Unfortunately, other European countries, particularly southern European states, are reluctant to take up e-commerce. The OECD is currently investigating measures to narrow the information technology gap between small companies in the EU and the US. The US economy continues to grow steadily, driven principally by new technologies — notably the Internet.

European businesses, with the correct strategic fit for e-commerce, should prepare now for the post-millennial boom in Internet-based trading. E-commerce is set to explode after the millennium, when other IT concerns, such as the "millennium bug" are dealt with. It is thus especially important that small businesses establish an Internet-based brand for themselves in order to secure an early market share in their specific market sector. Once rival companies are established it will be very difficult to displace them or compete effectively.

THE INTERNET

There is no one network known as *the Internet.* The Internet (or Net) is made up of many regional networks that are interconnected into one global network allowing communication in real-time. It is an *open* network; anybody can be part of it. No one company, organisation, or body owns the Internet. The networks that constitute the Internet are based within, or are provided by, telecommunications and software companies, academic institutions, government departments and agencies, public and private companies and individuals based at home. The information on the Internet flows across many types of communications media, from copper-wire telephone lines and fibre-optic cable to satellite dishes and cable.

Information can pass through all those different delivery systems because, at some point in its transmission, it has been converted to a common form: digital data. Any digital data or information has been converted to a signal made up of only the "digits" 0s and 1s. The vast amounts of information flowing throughout these networks all do so using one common global standard protocol, namely the Transmission Control Protocol/Internet Protocol (TCP/IP). Any computer can be connected to the Internet if it runs the TCP/IP protocol stack, has an IP (Internet Protocol) address, and has the ability to send IP packets to all the other machines on the Internet.[5] The IP address allows any Internet computer to talk to any other. Any recently manufactured computer system will be "Internet-ready".

ELECTRONIC COMMERCE

Electronic commerce (e-commerce) is a general concept that covers any form of business transaction that is conducted electronically using telecommunications networks, including the Internet. Such transactions occur between two or more companies, between companies and their customers or between companies and public administrations.

E-commerce encompasses a broad range of activities. It includes electronic trading of physical goods and services and of electronic material, including the advertising and promotion of products and services and the facilitation of contacts between traders. E-commerce is a concept combining all topics related to making business possible through the use of computer systems by both sellers and buyers.

E-commerce is therefore a mix of business processes and enabling technologies. Businesses and trading partners can become linked regardless of which sector they operate in. Use of e-commerce technologies is increasingly becoming a condition of business-to-business trading imposed by large customers, especially in the retail, manufacturing and automotive sectors. At the application level typical e-commerce technologies would include:

- Advertising and marketing
- Electronic funds transfer (EFT)
- Electronic data interchange (EDI)
- Electronic mail
- Voice messaging
- Electronic catalogues
- Technical data interchange
- Electronic forms
- Workflow
- Fax.

The activities we will concentrate on in this book will be Internet commerce — the advertising, marketing and selling of products and services from a web site.

There has been phenomenal growth in commercial presence on the Internet in recent times. The fastest growing, and most popular, part of the Internet is undoubtedly the hypermedia-based, graphically-oriented World Wide Web. The Web has become the commercial market of the Internet. Commercial growth of the Internet has increased by an estimated 10 to 13 per cent per month. In 1997 the Web became the sector with the most domain names (1,743,390), and it is estimated that it now has 65 per cent of all domain names (see Appendix 2). The number of web users is estimated to reach 320 million by the year 2000 and 720 million by 2005.

The Web has provided a new marketing medium and significantly enhanced information resources. Web utilisation can not only give a company an "Internet presence" from which to market its goods or services, but also provides opportunities to develop and expand new services. Innovative applications now exist that allow for sales and database interrogation to enhance a firm's marketing efficiency. There are other benefits too, such as e-mail and file transfer (FTP) functionality, providing improved internal and external communications.

Electronic commerce can be much more than just electronic shopping. In certain cases the process can go through the whole chain from pre-sales to delivery, payment and after-sales service. Everything but the physical delivery of goods can be done electronically, though many forms of services and information can be delivered digitally. Obviously, if the business relationship is intimate, some documents must be exchanged the traditional way, but after the mutual trust is created the need for that kind of action is reduced.

A business-to-business transaction typically involves a certain amount of documents and enquiries from both participants. When this is made via e-mail, it becomes part of electronic business. A business-to-customer transaction involves less information exchange and the products and services offered tend to be less complicated. Creating the consumer trust that is necessary for a consumer transaction is another subject that is dealt with in detail in the book (see Chapter 10, Attracting and Keeping Customers: Consumer Trust).

The Internet can reduce costs and help provide a higher level of customer care. Electronic communication and trading opportunities also offer some small businesses in particular the chance to compete for business on an international scale in a global market. The Internet now offers the prospect of an international, relatively inexpensive, and easily accessible advertising opportunity for small firms such as no media has ever offered before.

The Internet is now recognised as an essential resource by high-technology firms and major corporations due to their complex communications needs. However, managers of smaller firms question its relevance for them. If the Internet is a resource suited to a particular business operation then smaller companies *may*, but *only* may, stand to benefit from doing business on the Internet. Analysis of the potential competitive advantage that the Internet could provide in dealing with suppliers, the marketing and selling of goods and services, the revamping of internal operations, and enhancing relationships with customers, should help to determine the need for an Internet presence and the anticipated volume of Internet use by an organisation. This strategic evaluation should be conducted thoroughly before embarking on an Internet-based business venture.

STRATEGIC ANALYSIS

To assist in evaluating whether or not your specific proposed online business venture is likely to be successful trading on the Internet, the first section of this book, *Strategic Fit*, outlines the essential prerequisites for a business to be successful online. The section lists various opportunities for companies considering going online, including the advantages of business-to-business e-commerce. Finally, the section also details actual case studies of established online traders and those small firms considering going online. These case studies are then evaluated using a *Strategic Fit Matrix* which analyses specifically whether or not each individual company is likely to be successful trading online.

Provided you are confident that your business has the correct strategic fit for e-commerce, the second and third sections of the book — *Going On-line* and *Doing Business on the Internet* — outline the most cost-effective and efficient ways in which to set-up, market and maintain a commercial web site.

References

1. *Creating a Favourable Business Environment for Electronic Commerce: The European Approach.* http://europe.eu.int/comm/dg03/speeches/sm980225.htm

2. www.mori.com. "UK Entrepreneurs Are Getting Connected: Surveys Reveal Increasing Take Up of E-Commerce".

3. 13 April, 1999

4. *Computing*, 8 April, 1999, p. 27

5. Roche, B. (Minister for Small Business) *Financial Mail on Sunday*, 12 July 1998

6. Tanenbaum, A.S., *Computer Networks*, 3rd ed. (Prentice Hall International Ltd.: London) 1996, pp 35-38.

Part 1

Strategic Fit

2

STRATEGIC EVALUATION

"The Internet is like a telephone. You can't just plug it in and expect a business return" (Heather Starck, Principal Consultant, Ovum Consulting, 1998).[1]

There are increasing amounts of Internet facilities and "solutions" available for use by small businesses, all of which promise strategic and competitive advantage and improved efficiency. However, unlike large organisations who can subsidise developing new business ventures, small businesses with "resource poverty" have to make critical decisions to justify the financial and opportunity costs of computerising their business and building a Web presence.

The main objective of this book is to attempt to establish the cost-effectiveness of implementing Internet facilities, for what may be an investment requiring a large percentage of a firm's total budget and a fundamental revision of company strategy. Regardless of the capability and efficiency of Internet solutions now available for small businesses, it is the suitability of those applications to the needs of each specific business that is the realistic criterion for the implementation of Internet solutions; this is *strategic logic*.[2]

Strategic logic refers to the matching of the activities of an organisation to its environment.[3] Small businesses are likely to be operating in a single market, or a limited range of markets, probably with a limited range of products or services. It is likely that, unless the firm is specialising in some particular market segment, it will be subject to significant competitive pressures, so issues of competitive strategy are likely to be especially significant for the small firm.

Strategic evaluation (i.e. rational and economic assessments to determine which strategic direction a company should take) is primarily concerned with matching a company's specific strategic options with that company's market placement and its relative strategic capabilities or core competences. This rationale is the basis of strategic logic, and should help determine which businesses have the suitable "strategic fit" for e-commerce.

STRATEGIC FIT

Strategic fit is the state in which the activities of an organisation match the environment in which it conducts commerce. For a small business owner-manager, evaluating whether or not their particular business has the correct strategic fit for Internet commerce will be the most critical judgement they must make. Small businesses are likely to operate with a limited range of products or services aimed at an equally limited range of customers. Small firms are also likely to be subject to significant financial and competitive pressures, so issues of competitive strategy and investment decisions are likely to be critical to the success or failure of those small firms.

Internet service providers (ISPs), Internet software producers, and the Internet-related industry in general, would have all businesses, regardless of size, believe that not to be on the Internet is to commit commercial suicide. The Internet industry would never promote the fact that the Internet has such a small and demographically narrow audience that, for many small businesses, an Internet presence is at best a waste of money and at worst a crippling financial burden.

Determining the strategic direction your company should take means matching what you want to sell and where you want to sell it (*strategic aims*) with who you want to sell it to (*market placement*). In other words, do people in that segment want what you are selling? These evaluations will determine whether your business has the suitable strategic fit for Internet commerce (i.e. is your target market on the Net?).

Multinationals and larger companies, especially modern, high-tech or prestigious, image-conscious organisations, need an Internet presence as a status symbol or as another marketing tool; a small part of their overall marketing campaign. However, small businesses cannot afford a web site for the sake of corporate vanity.

The fact is that the Internet audience is, at present, extremely limited in terms of the range of prospective customers, and even more limited are the regular cash-paying purchasers of Internet goods and services that companies must target in order to be profitable.* If the product or service your company has to offer does not appeal to the current Internet audience then setting up an Internet presence at present will only serve as a frustrating drain of your company's cash.

A survey by CommerceNet at the end of 1998 estimated that there were around 80 million people on the World Wide Web. This might seem encouraging, but the overwhelming majority of these early adopters are American, English-speaking,† single males, aged between 20 and 35, well educated, and high earners (see Appendix 1). All subsequent surveys constantly confirm these findings.

Though the size of the net audience has continued to grow, the demographics have remained the same. Therefore, this demog-

---

* e-commerce accounts for less than 1 per cent of all EU commerce.

† Sixty per cent of current Internet users are American and 80 per cent of the Internet is in English.

raphically narrow audience should be the most profitable consumer target group for Internet commerce. Bluntly, if your company does not provide a product or service that consistently appeals to this specific group of consumers then it has little chance
of ever being profitable.

Small businesses are increasingly tempted by the prospect of e-
commerce, but what works on the High Street may not win trade
on the Web. The Internet does have the potential to reach vast
audiences, allowing truly international commerce, and provide
the biggest change in world trade this century and become the
world's biggest shopping centre. However, an unsound commercial idea will flounder regardless of its medium and in Cyberspace
this is even more crucial.

Consideration should be made as to whether your ideas are
commercially sound and whether they will appeal to (or "fit") the
audience on the Web. The economic advantages are straightforward: entry to the sector does not have to be expensive and there
exists increasingly wide market coverage for businesses offering
high-demand goods and services; also, the first company to establish a new market sector invariably gains the largest share of
that market. However, careful consideration should be made for
those businesses offering goods and services that do not appeal to
the limited Internet audience. It is particularly true for small businesses that can least afford an ill-directed corporate strategy.

ADDING VALUE

If a company has the strategic fit for e-commerce, and provides
products or services that appeal to the Internet audience, it should
endeavour to gain and maintain competitive advantage over its
rivals through "adding value" to the products or services it provides. Assuming that your product or service is not wholly
unique, why should a customer purchase what you have to offer
rather than buy from your competitors? Any competitive advan-

tage will be gained from the extra value added to your product or service, and will be maintained through developing a buyer-seller relationship. These measures will hopefully result in long-term customer loyalty.

The two main reasons Internet users give for using the Net are information (52 per cent) and entertainment (46 per cent). There-fore, information and entertainment are excellent added-value content for any web site. The value you add to the product or service you provide should also create a more pleasurable experi-ence for your customers by providing some of the following:

- Entertainment
- Information
- Product knowledge
- Advice
- After-sales service
- Free gifts
- Free memberships
- Discounts
- Free links to other sites, etc.

Customers also derive added-value from the purchasing experi-ence, such as:

- Simple, easy-to-understand order forms
- An attractive or fashionable web site environment
- Being made to feel as if they are a valued customer, i.e. the "feel-good" factor (see Chapter 10, Attracting and Keeping Customers: Customer Service and Value-added Selling).

BUSINESS STRUCTURE

An Internet-based business structure should be as efficient as any form of commercial venture, with effective commercial systems supporting its "shop front". Any e-commerce business should be based on a 20 per cent technology/80 per cent customer priority ratio. Commerce is about customers not technology. The front-end (customer interface) should be supported by a back-end (business structure) with all relevant information passing freely between the two.

An efficient business structure, in terms of its integration of Internet-related infrastructure and channels to market, is essential if it is to cope in the fast-moving virtual environment of e-commerce. Successful e-commerce should provide a number of access methods seamlessly integrated into the core architecture, without conflicting with or cannibalising the existing customer base.

An online business should offer customers at least the same service levels they expect in the High Street. For example, if security, efficiency, convenience, customer service or delivery speeds are not comparable to the real world, why should customers purchase in the virtual world? Customer care, such as e-mail order confirmation and complaint handling, can create profitable customer loyalty and competitive advantage. It is often service and support that set firms apart and become their USP (unique selling point).

Internet users are used to an instant, real-time environment. They therefore expect an equally fast response time to any orders they may make. Any online business should try to provide quick, easy-to-use and efficient payment systems (such as real-time credit card transaction systems), but if you have to handle transactions manually, that create delivery delays, then the customer should be informed. Also, customer dialogue should be maintained whenever necessary.

Everything sold has to be delivered. Reliable delivery systems should be in place before trading commences. Shipping costs vary according to weight, size and destination. Actual shipping costs to most areas of the world should be calculated and displayed on your online order forms. If calculations are not made before shipping, they may cost more than estimated, thus reducing profit. Any large or difficult to handle product may incur extra costs, also reducing profit margins. The extra delivery costs, such as import tax and VAT, incurred by the customer may also prohibit your sales.

Some online shop-building packages offer calculation applications and international courier companies (e.g. DHL and TNT) offer similar account facilities. The long-term solution will be to improve delivery services so that an increasingly wide range of goods can be delivered out of normal working hours. A 24-hour delivery system is needed to match the 24-hour ordering system the Internet provides.

If you do not have all the above elements in place before you commence online trading you will struggle to keep any hard-won customers due to their discontent with your service. And remember: It is cheaper to retain existing customers than to attract new ones. If your web site is to become successful, and customer traffic increases, it will be the business issues that will determine its continued popularity. Most successful e-commerce is about target marketing and efficient distribution channels. Few customers will go to a site they know nothing about, or return to one without continuous availability and fast response times.

You should evaluate all these considerations before building a commercial web site. As with all commercial projects, the key to success is planning. Whatever the reasoning, an Internet presence should be based on realistic strategies and objectives and, most importantly, it should possess the correct strategic fit for e-commerce.

WHAT WORKS ON THE INTERNET

So which businesses actually have the correct "fit" for Internet commerce? The obvious candidates for successful e-commerce are simple, recognisable products or services that are easily understood. If the product or service is well understood, the next thing to consider is whether your target market fits the profile of the largely English-speaking and American web audience.

If an idea is original, or a new direction for an existing product, or is a service with considerable human involvement, or something complicated to understand, people may be suspicious and unwilling to take the risk of purchase. If a company has to offer some form of pre-sales service to explain the benefits of what they offer, then they may need to continue their existing practice of taking orders over the phone or by post, rather than conduct transactions over the Net. There is also little sense in a small firm with limited facilities and resources offering generic local services, such as plumbing, baking or decorating, and hoping to sell them on the Web.

The following list highlights those Internet promotions which do *not* have the strategic fit for e-commerce:

- Offers generic products or services freely available, and as easily obtainable, elsewhere.

- Does not appeal to the limited web audience.

- Disregards the customers' needs and is limited by its geographical range.

- Annoys customers with uninteresting information.

- Strains customers' equipment with injudicious use (or overuse) of Internet technology.

- Misjudges the value customers give to a product.

- Fails to enhance the product or service with added value and information.

If your company decides to go online and you have formulated an Internet-related business plan, consideration should be made as to what risks you are willing to take and how you are going to measure your company's success against its objectives. The costs involved in trading over the Net range significantly, therefore you have to evaluate how much you can afford to spend. However, if your products or services fit the consumer profile of the net audience then you may well enjoy excellent profitability.

Most research evidence suggests that, broadly speaking, there are three ways to make money from a company web site:

1. The marketing of goods or services.

2. The selling of advertising. Some sites are managing to do this even now, but they rely on being established brands with a guaranteed high hit rate, such as the search engine sites, or sites that are straight conversions of big-name print titles.

3. Conducting all of a company's transactions on the Web. For example, an Internet-based music company may procure music downloaded directly from an artist, market it, sell it, receive payment for it and deliver it directly to the purchaser — all conducted over the Internet.

CHECKLIST

The following list highlights which Internet-based promotions have the correct strategic fit for e-commerce:

- Appeals to the demographically narrow web audience.

- Identifies which products, services, entertainment, or information customers are *really* interested in; provides a genuinely useful product or service.

- Establishes a buyer-seller relationship and customer loyalty.

- Uses technology judiciously.

- Focuses on customers' convenience and being user-friendly.

- Provides an exclusive, bespoke or specialised product or service.

- Saves the customer money.

- Provides products or services that are difficult to acquire elsewhere.

- Adds value, i.e. provides information about products or services, or entertains customers, or makes the purchasing process more pleasurable.

- Has the structures in place (such as a delivery system) to cope efficiently with any potential demand.

References

[1] *Computing*, 6 November 1998, p. 20

[2] Johnson, G. & Scholes, K. *Exploring Corporate Strategy: Text and Cases*, 3rd ed. Prentice Hall Europe: London. 1993, p. 248

[3] Ibid. p. 6.

3

SMALL BUSINESS OPPORTUNITIES ON THE INTERNET

As with all new markets, and new media, it is the first to market that captures the largest market share. As each new successful Internet-related market sector is discovered others quickly exploit it. When a market sector nears saturation, to compete in that sector it becomes necessary for smaller firms to specialise or target a niche market sector directly. According to most reports books, CDs, holidays, tickets, computers and software are the consumer items most in demand over the Internet (see Appendix 8). These and other successful Internet-based businesses and promotion ideas are analysed below:

- Adult checks
- Advertorials
- Auctions
- Banner advertising
- Bit products
- Book sales
- Bounties
- Brokering
- Charging for access
- Collectables
- Computer supplies
- Computer manufacture
- Contents provision
- Consultancy
- Contest hosting
- Contra deals
- E-mailing lists
- Graphic art
- Internet Service Provider (ISP)

- Link sales
- Music sales
- Selling highly customised products
- Selling other people's products
- Selling tickets
- Sex sites
- Shareware
- Shareware Hosting

- Site hosting
- Software engineering
- Souvenir sales
- Specialised goods and services
- Sponsorships
- Surveys
- Travel
- Value-added Information Services

ADULT CHECKS

If the content of your web site is even slightly "adult", it can probably join one of the age-verification schemes, such as AdultCheck (www.adultcheck.com).[1] There are about eight of these in existence, and they all work on the same basis. A visitor fills in their credit card details and pays $10 (£6 or €9.50) for a year's membership, for which they can then gain access to all member sites. If anybody joins the scheme from your company's site, AdultCheck will pay you up to $7.50 (£5 or €7) of that $10 (see Sex Sites).

ADVERTORIALS

There are a growing number of web sites that will advertise a company's products or services in exactly the same way as magazines, local newspapers or telephone directories etc. advertise local businesses. The only difference is that the adverts used are banners, text, graphics or photos (exactly the same as are used in paper publications) but are placed on web pages rather than paper pages. For many micro-businesses this may represent the cheapest way for them to initiate an Internet presence or market themselves on the web.

AUCTIONS

Online auctions, such as uBid (www.ubid.com), where companies sell their stock to the highest bidder, are quickly becoming very popular on the Net. Online auctions such as these are particularly popular with the young Internet audience who are looking for electrical and electronic consumer goods. Currently, Europe's largest online auctioneer is Quixell (www.quixell.com), but there are an increasing amount of localised auction sites appearing (see Chapter 6, Case Studies: *eBid*).

BANNER ADVERTISING

Ad banners are small rectangular advertising images, which appear on an increasing number of web sites. The Internet Advertising Bureau (www.iab.net) sets the standard size for banners at 468 pixels wide x 60 pixels deep. This is not a legal standard but has been agreed by the US and most EU countries (see Plate 3.1).

PLATE 3.1: TOYOTA BANNER AD

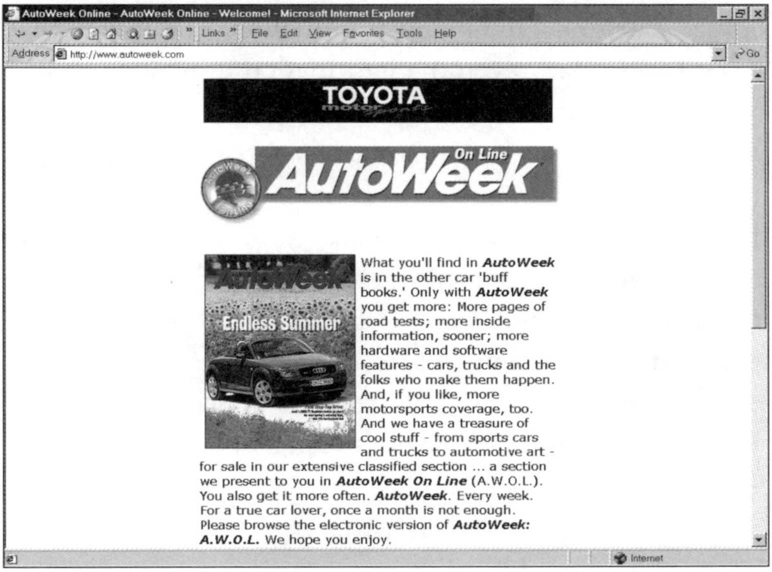

At the moment, 63 per cent of all the cash spent on banner ads goes to just the top 10 web sites, but the market was £69 million (€107 million) last year and is expected to grow to over £250 million (€387 million) by the year 2000. Banner advertisements are usually paid for on an "impressions" basis; every time a banner is displayed another impression is notched up as well as another potential client.

If your web site receives a large amount of visitor traffic, other companies may want to advertise on your site. If you have your site audited by a respected online auditor, who can supply a certificate to prove the large amount of traffic you receive, then you are more likely to attract advertising from large, and profitable, corporations.

BIT PRODUCTS

"Bit products" refers to the concept that everything, goods as well as services, can be thought of as either "atoms" or "bits" (Negroponte 1996).[2] *Atoms* are physical, tangible products and *bits* are conceptual, electronic, intangible information. The Internet world is moving toward bits, even the information previously delivered as books, memos, and letters (all atoms) are now increasingly available as documents on the computer screen or web pages (all bits).

Bit products are clearly particularly suitable for electronic trading. Due to the electronic delivery of products, the whole chain can be automated, except the manufacturing of physical products. This means low set-up and transaction costs for the seller. Information and services, such as consultancy, delivered over the Net is a good example of the concept of a bit product.

BOOK SALES

Books sell well on the Internet because they are comparatively inexpensive and customers know what they are going to get for their money. However, your company's site does not need to be a bookseller in order to sell them. Several of the big web booksellers offer "partnership" programmes for other sites where a company provides an ordering button on its site linked to a publisher's site containing books relevant to whatever the company's site is promoting. The publisher then handles all the order processing and fulfilment, and pays a percentage of the cover price as a commission.

The Internet Bookshop (www.bookshop.co.uk) for example, has nearly a million titles for sale. When a company becomes an Internet Bookshop (iBS) partner it can choose the particular titles it wants to sell or let visitors choose from any of its titles. iBS takes all the orders, handles all customer questions and requests (including cancellations and returns) and then packages and ships any book order anywhere in the world. The company then sends the bill to the customer, collects the cash, and hands over a portion of the fee to the partner company.

Other companies, which offer a similar scheme, include Bookpages (www.bookpages.co.uk) and Amazon (www.amazon.com). Amazon is the world's largest bookshop and has over 2.5 million titles. It was the first Internet retailer to reach the one-millionth new customer in October 1997. The success story of Amazon began in 1995 when Founder and CEO Jeff Bezos started Amazon.com out of his garage, wrapping orders and delivering them to the post office.

There is no reason why owner-managers of small businesses should not make a success of book selling online, providing they identify a niche market to target. Obscure or specialist books can be difficult to acquire and take up to six weeks to be delivered. This fact provides an opportunity for specialist bookshops, such as Watkin's Books (www.watkinsbooks.com). Watkin's Books specialise in books on the mind, body and spirit. What differentiates the company from others in this market is its specialist, detailed knowledge and expertise in sourcing obscure titles (see Plate 3.2).

PLATE 3.2: WATKIN'S BOOKS

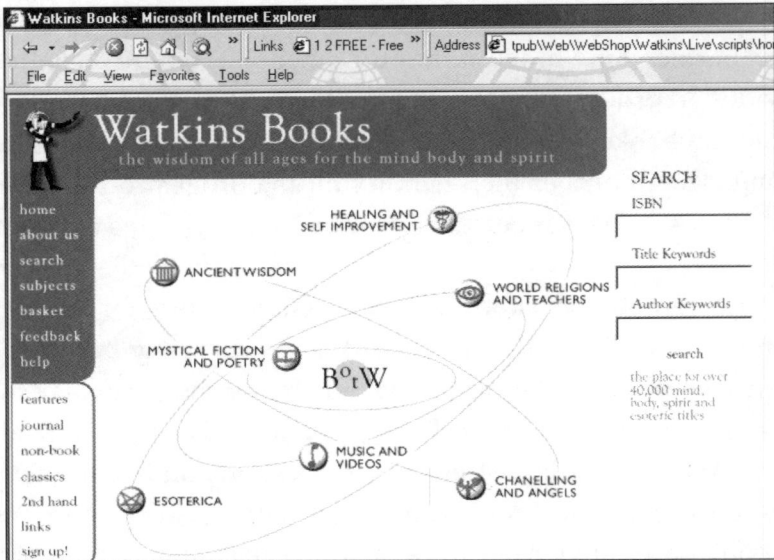

BOUNTIES

As used in the direct marketing industry, this concept is similar to a simple finder's fee. Sites such as www.elibrary.com charge a premium for access to the most comprehensive areas of information. If your company points potential customers in their direction, they will pay you a commission on that fee. Your company also has the added benefit of getting content for use on your own site.

BROKERING

Brokering of anything on the Internet would appear to be a good business opportunity. Typically, the broker does not have any stock, does not own the merchandise, and the transaction is made between the selling and buying parties. The broker facilitates the deal, acts as a consultant for both parties, and takes care of the possible paperwork.

Travel is already the biggest selling product on the Internet, and if the trend continues more than £292 million (€452 million) worth of air travel will be booked by Europeans on the Internet by 2002.[3] Most web-based travel agents use the *Sabre* booking system, which gives information on flight availability and lowest fares.[4] According to a report by Datamonitor, travel will account for 35 per cent of all online sales by the year 2002.[5] The dramatic increase from 7 per cent in 1997 to 20 per cent in 1999 reflects the suitability of the travel industry as the perfect Internet business[6] (see Travel below).

Insurance is another brokering service well suited to the Internet. Well known insurers such as Eagle Star have started low-cost travel insurance from its web site.[7] Drivers can now use one-stop web sites to shop around for the best car insurance deals. The first European site to offer such services was Screentrade (www.screentrade.com), which offers free brokerage services, saving time and broker's charges. Home insurance and others will soon follow.[8]

One of the traditional brokering industries, real estate, is beginning to establish a presence on the Internet. An advantage of the Net, besides significant cost savings, is its greater geographical reach. Conveyancing Direct Ltd (www.convey ancingdirect.co.uk) was the first company in Europe to enable the total conveyancing process to take place over the Web.[9] The property market is another area hoping to attract homeowner's advertising.[10]

It could be assumed that many business opportunities for brokerage businesses exist on the Net that have yet to be exploited.

CHARGING FOR ACCESS

If your company's web site contains valuable content it can password-protect part of its site and charge a fee to access that information (see Plate 3.3).

PLATE 3.3: ENCYCLOPAEDIA BRITANNICA ONLINE

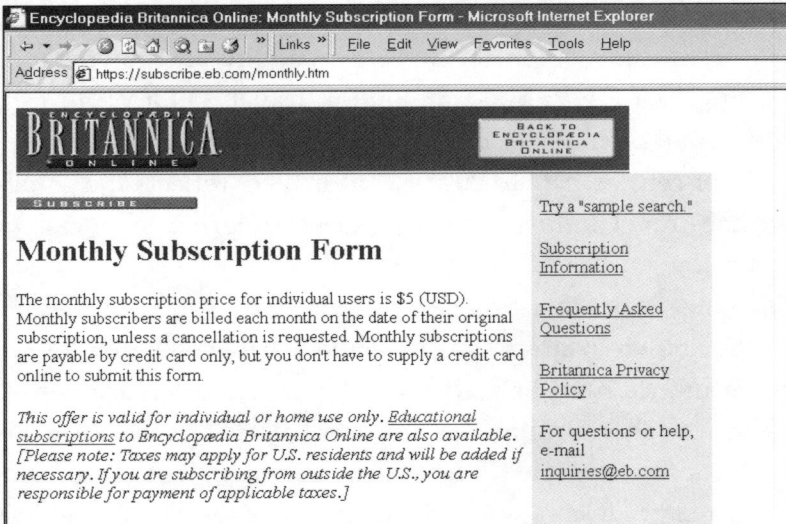

Encyclopædia Britannica Online: Monthly Subscription Form - Microsoft Internet Explorer

Address https://subscribe.eb.com/monthly.htm

BRITANNICA
ONLINE

BACK TO
ENCYCLOPÆDIA
BRITANNICA
ONLINE

SUBSCRIBE

Monthly Subscription Form

The monthly subscription price for individual users is $5 (USD). Monthly subscribers are billed each month on the date of their original subscription, unless a cancellation is requested. Monthly subscriptions are payable by credit card only, but you don't have to supply a credit card online to submit this form.

This offer is valid for individual or home use only. Educational subscriptions to Encyclopædia Britannica Online are also available. [Please note: Taxes may apply for U.S. residents and will be added if necessary. If you are subscribing from outside the U.S., you are responsible for payment of applicable taxes.]

Try a "sample search."

Subscription Information

Frequently Asked Questions

Britannica Privacy Policy

For questions or help, e-mail inquiries@eb.com

COLLECTABLES

There is a large and growing market for collectables on the Net. Small niche businesses, as well as individuals, are using the huge global web network to reach a far larger percentage of interested customers. Antiques, as specialised goods appealing to a specific niche market, should sell well, although the young, male Internet audience does not tend to be interested in antiques. However, similar items that do appeal to them (i.e. collectables) do tend to sell well: stamps, sports and military memorabilia sell particularly well, e.g. North East Militaria & Supplies (www.btinternet. com/ ~ne.mas/) (see Chapter 6, Case Studies: *North East Militaria & Suppliers* and *Trophy Miniatures of Wales*). In Europe, football memorabilia is particularly in demand — everything from rare programmes to replica shirts are considered collector's items. Programmes are the most popular collectable but rare or old photographs are also valuable collector's items.

COMPUTER SUPPLIES

Being a computer-based industry, any related products have obvious appeal to the online audience. Most of these computer-literate, Internet-familiar consumers like to keep up with the latest computer technology. Therefore, for consumers to upgrade their computers, there is a constant demand for the latest hardware and software products. Any online company that specialises in a specific sector of the home PC, business or computer games markets should see a demand for its goods.

COMPUTER MANUFACTURE

Building a computer is easier than it has ever been. It is relatively straightforward to get hold of the components, and because you are making it yourself it works out quite economical. It is no surprise then that many people are now building and selling PCs for a living, undercutting major manufacturers who have to meet much higher overheads and transport costs. Competitive advantage could be gained through offering a bespoke online service offering machines built to the specific specifications of the buyer (see Selling Highly Customised Products below).

CONSULTANCY

There are thousands of companies offering consultancy services of every kind over the Net. From art to web design, most knowledge or skill-based talents are represented on the Web. At present, the most successful are Internet-related consultants, such as Web masters. Once your company has been set up online you may then be able to sell your expertise and experience to other companies operating in the same field.

For example, to develop a competitive web site requires three kinds of specialised skills:

1. *Content Providers* to devise and provide the content, information and entertainment on the web pages.

2. *Graphic Designers* to construct the graphics; to lure the viewer and to design the look of the site.

3. *Technology Providers* to write the scripts and transfer text contents to a hypertext format.

These roles can be, and often are, mixed. Because all three assets seldom reside in the same company, there is an opportunity for "netrepreneurs" to exploit the shortage of these much-in-demand skills. It is technically simple to outsource one or all of these tasks. This opportunity has created numerous multimedia companies that produce and maintain web sites.

CONTEST HOSTING

Competitions attract visitors to web sites (e.g. www.theinternet raffle.com). By setting up a web site competition, third party companies, who may or may not have a web presence, may buy the e-mail addresses of those visitors to the web site competition. Companies such as iMusic (www.imusic.com) host contests, competitions and surveys to attract customers. To enter a competition the user must give their personal details. A database of everybody who enters the site should be kept, which is not difficult to set up, and the list can then be sold to other companies.

CONTRA DEALS

Contra deals are a mainstay of the advertising world, and it is a common way of doing business on the Net. A company offers a service (this could be advertising space, or even a dedicated editorial) in exchange for goods and services rather than for direct payment. Both parties benefit without cost.

E-MAILING LISTS

If your company's site has a guest book, or you regularly receive e-mail feedback from your web site visitors, a database can be created from their e-mail addresses and then sold on to third party direct marketers.

GRAPHIC ART

Art, clip art, graphics, animation and cartoons are in great demand as web site managers seek to include added-value entertainment content to their sites. Due to the Web being a graphics-orientated medium, any design-based industry may be able to use its web site to advertise its design skills. For example, Card Corporation (www.cardcorp.co.uk) allows customers to design their own business cards online. Other companies, such as DJH Graphics (www.users.zetnet.co.uk/djh-graphics), offer a full graphic design service from their web site (see Chapter 6, Case Studies: *The Graphics Co.*).

INTERNET SERVICE PROVIDER (ISP)

The most successful Internet business is selling access.[11] ISPs do not offer their own content, but provide means to reach content. ISPs can be classified as telcos or cable companies, online services, national independents, regional and local providers. Local providers are commonly small businesses who can support from one to 10,000 users. They operate in one physical location and provide services within a single metropolitan area. Anyone can become an ISP. However, setting up an ISP may prove difficult, due to the saturation of this market sector and the economic barriers to entry,[12] but, theoretically at least, size should not be a prohibitive factor.

If a company or individual can identify or create a niche market, a strong brand or a unique selling point, then they may be able to compete profitably with the large established ISPs. Most ISPs provide a free access service, therefore the cost of a local call pays for the service, split between the telco, the phone link and you (the ISP). As an ISP, you will need to offer the Internet service, the phone link and technical support. Some companies, such as Telinco (www.telinco.net) and World CallNet (www.world-callnet.com), offer "virtual" ISP (VISP) packages where you can resell their service using your company name and, once you have gained a minimum number of calls or active users, you make a profit.

LINK SALES

A good way of generating repeat traffic is to have a list of links to other related sites. However, if that list becomes over-long, the number of visits each site can expect diminishes accordingly. It is a more cost-effective policy to link to the best, and most popular, sites. Space can then be sold on a "premium links" page to other sites; this is similar to a banner ad without the banner. Some companies (e.g. www.webstats.com) offer free services if you provide a link to their site.

MUSIC SALES

Similar to books, records, tapes and CDs seem well suited to the virtual marketspace. If your company's product can be translated to a digital format (a bit product), and your customer demographic matches that of most web users, then you can apply the e-commerce strategies of the music industry to help your company cut costs and increase revenue. On the Web, music buyers can read reviews and listen to sound samples before buying a new CD. Most buyers have to wait at least a day for delivery, but a growing number of customers record digitised songs directly off the Web. This knowledge can be adapted to any bit product.

The Web's impact on industries such as the recording industry and on music retailing is becoming more apparent. Music is well suited to web sales. The demographic targeting is excellent; the overlap of young CD buyers and web users. There now exists the technological ability to translate music, like software and print, into digital form, which can be sent over the Internet. This allows customers to download specific tracks rather than whole albums. MP3 technology, a Midi connection and FTP allow musicians to play, in real-time, with other musicians anywhere in the world, and record it.

Many in the business predict that when high-speed modems, recordable CD drives, and broadband Internet access become commonplace, the music buying experience, from ordering to fulfilment, is likely to be primarily an electronic transaction. Many analysts point to the music industry's online success as a model for other industries interested in leveraging the Web for business-to-consumer commerce.

CDnow Inc., the biggest online music retailer, was launched three years ago on a $20,000 (€18,900) investment. CDnow (www.cdnow.com) presently owns 33 per cent of the market, more than twice the share of its nearest competitor. And that market is growing fast. Currently at £14 million (€17 million) per year, compared with £7 billion (€11 billion) for all music retailing, Internet music retailing will be a £1.7 billion (€2.6 billion) business by 2002. Most observers agree that those labels likely to benefit most from web sales are smaller, niche labels, e.g. www.catapult.co.uk. (see Chapter 6, Case Studies: *Catapult 100 per cent Vinyl*).

SELLING HIGHLY CUSTOMISED PRODUCTS

In some cases all products manufactured by a small business can be highly customised. A product with a lot of customised options may be difficult to sell via traditional channels. If your product is highly customised or is a highly specialised item, and if the product is targeted to a very narrow audience, this may be very commercially successful online due to the huge potential market the Internet provides. Provided that your product will appeal to the young male Net audience then it may sell exceptionally well over the Web. (see Chapter 6, Case Studies: *Trophy Miniatures Wales Ltd.*)

Your company can provide an electronic catalogue designed to display all product options and allow the buyer to download and print an order form to be e-mailed or faxed to the company. The Net is also a good advertising tool for purchases that are handled with "absolute confidentiality and discretion" and for which the company guarantees "complete and total privacy". Male shoppers may also appreciate the anonymous ordering system. "Made-to-measure" items and "one-offs" are also likely to sell well as customers often surf the Net in hope of finding products that are unique or not readily available locally.

SELLING OTHER PEOPLE'S PRODUCTS

Certain reputable companies on the Internet will pay to have their banner advertisements displayed on your company's web site. Others will pay commission to your company for selling their products. Usually, a company will have had to have amassed a sufficient or fixed amount before a cheque is issued. The procedure for operating this is simple and costs nothing. Sites that suit a company's activities can be found at http://sky-l.com. Once the on-line registration form, and all codes, instructions etc. has been filled out, all relevant information will be forwarded.

SELLING TICKETS

Ticketmaster is Europe's largest online ticket seller.[13] Their 1998 ticket sales figures were in excess of 1 million tickets, with a total value of over £24 million (€37 million). Ticket sales of all kinds seem to be a business well suited to e-commerce, even for bookings requiring significant amounts, such as air tickets.[14] British Airways has so far sold £2 million (€3 million) worth of tickets through its online booking service.[15] This is an example of how the public are prepared to browse the Web if it results in cheaper prices, especially if the Internet gives customers access to the same data as any "middle man" or agent.[16]

SEX SITES

The undeniable reality of Internet commerce is that it is domi-
nated by sex; 70 per cent to 80 per cent of every hit is a search for
pornographic material. It should not be surprising that with a
huge audience of mostly young, single males, most Internet enquiries are sex-related. Gay or straight sex is one thing that this
demographic sector is guaranteed to have an interest in. Censor-
ship on the Net is minimal so the explicitness and diversity of sex
sites on the Web matches the appetite for it. There are currently an
estimated 1.5 million sex sites on the Internet. At present there is
an insatiable greed for Net pornography (see Chapter 10, Attracting and Keeping Customers: Sex Sells, and Appendix 5c).

SHAREWARE

The general idea behind shareware is that software is offered free
of charge for people to try before they commit themselves to a
purchase. Customers are only asked to pay for it if they continue
to find the product useful after a certain length of time.

Normally shareware is software, often a scaled-down version
of a full product, but it does not have to be. Reports and information, or any other kind of service, can be offered on a shareware
basis.

SHAREWARE HOSTING

Another option is to become a shareware site for other vendors by
agreeing to devote a small part of a site to the promotion of their
wares, in exchange for a percentage of any licensing fees sold (e.g.
www.samplenet.com). Becoming a recognised source of shareware may also work well in improving hit rates.

SITE HOSTING

If your company has a particularly attractive or trendy domain
name you can "leverage" it by offering related sites space on your

server. However, there may be tricky issues to resolve regarding passwords for FTP access, and the ISP might want to start charging for any excess space used, but the appeal of this scheme lies in the fact that, theoretically, it should guarantee a higher amount of customer traffic.

SOFTWARE ENGINEERING

Many computer programmers with skills in high-demand languages, such as Visual Basic, Java, C++ etc., now work freelance from home. Most promote their specialist programs through shareware and sell the code over the Internet. With so many sectors of the business community now taking up computer-based commercial systems, there is an increasing demand for various programs. A freelance software engineer who can produce specialised programs for niche market businesses can achieve extremely profitable global sales (see Bit Products and Shareware Hosting above).

SOUVENIRS SALES

If your company develops an attractive or trendy brand for its site it may be able to sell "quality merchandise" on the back of it. You may add your company's logo to T-shirts, mouse mats, mugs, pens and more. Many companies make more money from merchandising than from their original products or services.

SPECIALISED GOODS AND SERVICES

The opportunity to market specialist goods globally may become the small business's most common and successful approach to Internet commerce. Specialisation of products (e.g. left-handed goods) and services (e.g. bespoke software), whether to individual customers or business-to-business, may provide Internet entrepreneurs with profitable niche markets.

There are already many examples of small specialist companies doing good business on the Internet. Teddington Cheese (www.

teddingtoncheese.co.uk), a High Street cheese shop, has expanded its business globally by selling its specialist cheeses over the Net! Plade (www.plade.com), a specialist plastics company, has tripled its export since introducing its e-commerce web site.

The Smoke Shop (www.thesmokeshop.com) is a successful on-line shop that specialises in only one specific product: cigars. This particular product fits the profile of the online audience (used mainly by affluent males) and has the added advantage of being something that, due to the US embargo of Cuban imports, is something that can be difficult to obtain outside the Internet.

SPONSORSHIPS

Securing a sponsor for your site may make you money or help pay the cost of your Internet presence. As little as £25 (€39) a week from a sponsor may be all that is required to cover the costs of your web site, thus making all revenue gained clear profit. Hosting a sponsorship banner, or stating that your web site is sponsored by a specific company, may provide that company with all the Internet exposure they require. Also, reciprocal sponsorship may be worth pursuing with a complimentary company.

PLATE 3.4: SPONSORSHIPS

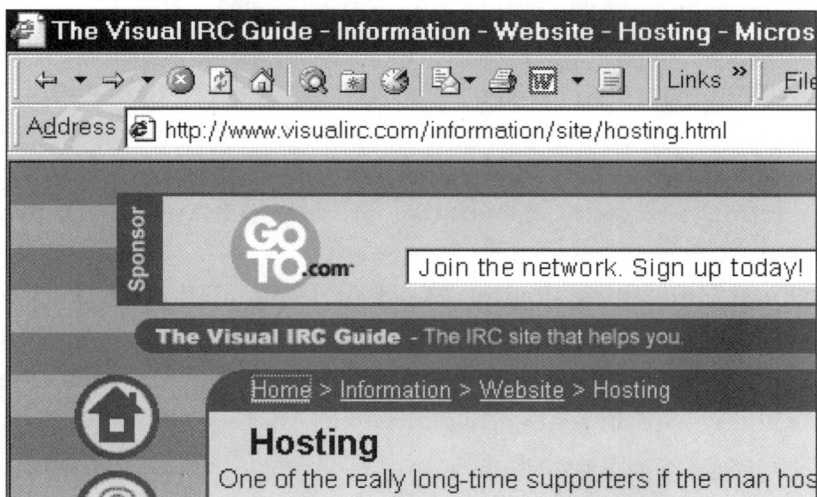

SURVEYS

There are two ways of making cash from surveys or market reports:

1. Your company can either charge a fee to another company for including your survey on its pages.

2. You can conduct your own survey and then sell the results to other companies that are interested in your web site visitors (e.g. www.epoll.com).

TRAVEL

In only a few years the online travel industry has already become a crowded market. Airline tickets, online booking services, online car hire reservations, package holidays, tourist information, hotel and restaurant reviews, menus, prices and weather forecasting are all services offered on the Web. Companies such as Bargain Holidays (www.bargainholidays.com), Flight Bookers (www.flight bookers.com) and Easy Jet (www.easyjet.com) have been quick to exploit a very fast-moving sector of the Internet.

The very competitive nature of the travel industry means that consumers are now used to "shopping around" for deals on holidays and flights. Hence the popularity of companies such as Last Minute (www.lastminute.com — see Plate 3.5). However, only the larger companies can realistically offer cheap deals. Therefore, as the market nears saturation, any small business entering this sector should focus on specialisation and developing niche markets and perhaps targeting the affluent and Internet-familiar countries such as America, Japan and Germany.

Small companies such as Heart of England Promotions Ltd. (www. heartofengland.co.uk), who specialise in themed and promotional events, have witnessed an increased demand from all over the world since advertising online. Another company, Sykes Cottages (www.sykescottages.co.uk), has doubled its booking response rate since advertising its holiday cottage rental business online.

PLATE 3.5: WWW.LASTMINUTE.COM

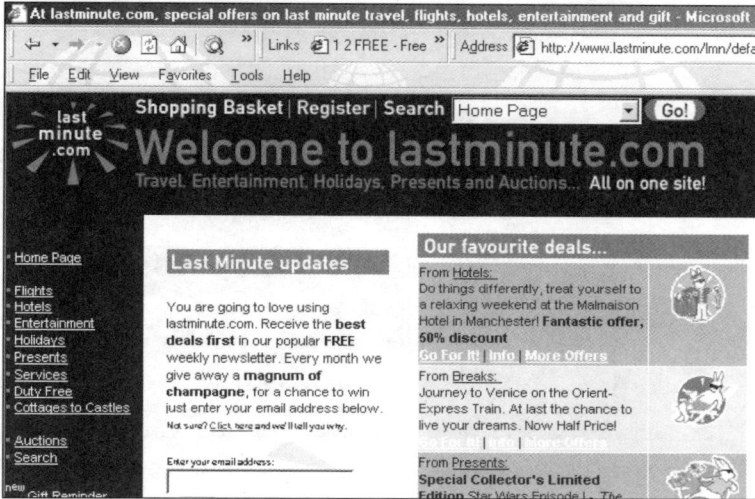

VALUE-ADDED INFORMATION SERVICES

Information brokers, or those companies specialising in knowledge-based services rather than in retail sales or manufacturing, is very likely to see little advantage in an Internet presence. However, these businesses *could* benefit from promoting their firms on the Internet through value-added information services. For example, solicitors, analysts, engineers, scientists, or tax consultants can offer customers updates and general advice on tax law changes etc.

For example, Desktop Lawyer (www.desktoplawyer.net — see Plate 3.6) offers a complete online legal service. Visitors to their site can download and assemble professionally drafted legal documents, such as standard legal letters and wills, all of which are then customised offline. The incentives for users are its speed, convenience and cost — savings of up to 90 per cent compared to High Street solicitors' fees.

PLATE 3.6: DESKTOP LAWYER

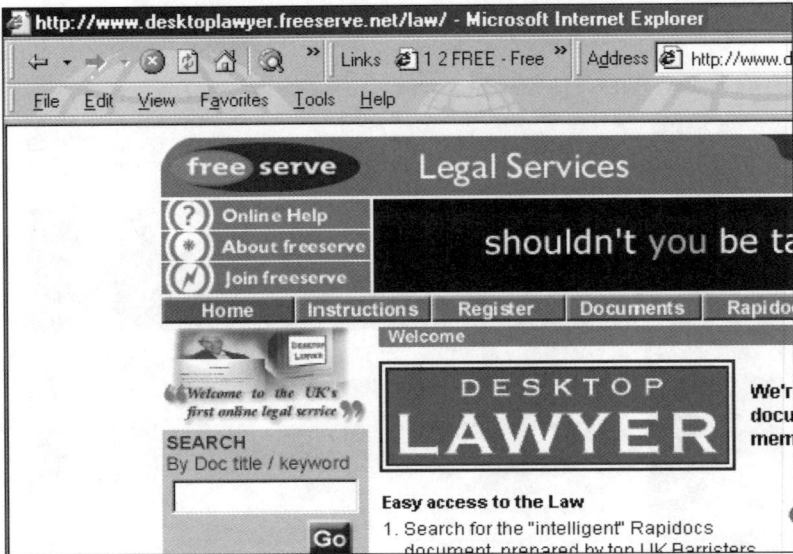

For knowledge-based services, providing some advice, such as updates, may be offered free but any in-depth or specific advice should be charged for. Any promotional material used to advertise such services should include credibility-building devices, CVs, client testimonials, and any relevant articles etc. and targeted at the right audience. Information-based businesses such as these can make excellent revenue when targeted at specific industries requiring specific, detailed information.

N.B. Many of the above opportunities can be used in combination within a company's commercial web site to add value to its web site and hopefully create a profitable ongoing revenue stream.

References

[1] www.adultcheck.com

[2] Negroponte, Nicholas (1996): *Being Digital*. Random House. http://www.obs-us.com:80/obs/eng-lish/books/nn/bdintro.htm

[3] *Financial Mail on Sunday*, 20 September 1998, p 43

[4] www.travelocity.com

[5] www.datamonitor.com

[6] *Internet Works Magazine*, Issue 8, Summer 1998, p 14

[7] www.eaglestardirect.co.uk

[8] www.eaglestar.co.uk

[9] www.conveyancingdirect.co.uk

[10] www.propertymarket.co.uk

[11] Kalakota, Ravi & Whinston, Andrew B. (1997): *Electronic Commerce — A Manager's Guide*. Addison-Wesley, pp. 38-40

[12] Johnson, G. & Scholes, K. *Exploring Corporate Strategy: Text and Cases*, 3rd ed. Prentice Hall Europe: London. 1993, p 88

[13] www.ticketmaster.co.uk

[14] *Internet Works Magazine*, Issue 7, July 1998, p 42

[15] www.british-airways.com

[16] www.abtanet.com.

4

BUSINESS-TO-BUSINESS INTERNET COMMERCE

The European e-commerce market, estimated at £128 million (€200 million) in 1998, is predicted to grow to £327 million (€510 million) by the end of 1999 and $4,000 billion (€3,800 billion) by 2004. This will happen mainly because SMEs will see the vast potential of the Internet and will start selling to each other online. Six out of ten European companies now buy and sell products over the Internet. Therefore, if small businesses are to be competitive in the future, they should be aware of e-commerce even if they do not have the ideal strategic fit for business-to-customer commerce. Certain business operations may well be perfectly suited to business-to-business e-commerce.

Whereas Internet surveys portray users as representing a narrow demographic cross-section and concern themselves mainly with the web audience of potential customers, the most influential users of the Internet are the businesses themselves that have connections to the Net. These are the organisations that have already been enhancing links with business customers and suppliers, cutting costs through competitive bidding and selling direct, without middlemen margins pushing prices to extremes. If the experts have it right, the Internet may go a long way toward meeting all business-to-business requirements as well as facilitating the global reach and flexible alliances that will become integral to modern commerce.

The size of the Internet presents opportunities for any business serious about expanding its marketing efforts to other businesses. The *Internet Marketing and Technology Report 1998* states that 42 per cent of web usage is work-related. For business-to-business marketers, the Web means more than mere visibility however; it also means the ability to offer wholesale catalogues that never go out-of-date and brochures that do not have to be mailed.

A benchmark already exists in the realm of non-Internet electronic commerce. The amount of merchandise purchased electronically by businesses (through EDI, e-mail and proprietary order entry) is 100 times greater than that purchased electronically by consumers (i.e. home-shopping, online commercial networks and home bill-paying).

Few would dispute the power of the Net to assist in pre-purchase research and price comparisons. The savings in time may be at least as useful as the ability to search out low prices. Savings as high as 30 to 40 per cent for manufacturers may be achieved on their purchases in terms of hours reduced from the procurement process. Time may be saved from not having to go to printed materials and search for something compared to how long it takes to search online catalogues, be automatically transferred to a distributor, and then be able to interactively receive information and place an order directly.

Many European telcos are now following their US counterparts by buying into business-to-business e-commerce through joint ventures with software vendors. For example, Netscape is expecting its existing partnership with France Telecom to host private buying forums for groups such as manufacturers' suppliers as they predict this sector of e-commerce to expand dramatically.

There is no doubt that US companies have been doing most of the early running on the Internet, and have been first to exploit the opportunities in e-commerce and online services. But early adoption may not always be the wisest course, and it is possible that the emerging digital economy gives European companies an opportunity to generate productivity rates more akin to the US model.

According to recent figures from the OECD, e-commerce is about to enter its second stage, where delivery of products and services is supported by a purpose-built infrastructure, rather than cobbled together from existing systems. The Internet may be one vast global network, but the markets it reaches are highly diverse and require different support, distribution and marketing structures. Companies should prepare now for the global opportunities the Internet will provide for those firms suited to business-to-business e-commerce.

AUTOMATED PURCHASING

In the last few years vendors have begun to develop software for buying goods that allow large organisations to offer their employees intranet-based access to preferred supplier catalogues. Instead of having a complex chain of management to control what is bought, companies can introduce purchasing software allowing them direct trading with certain suppliers. These purchasing applications, such as *BuyerXpert* from Netscape, are often controlling the purchase of *indirect* goods and services which support a company's operation but do not contribute to its revenues. Stationery and computer equipment are examples of indirect goods.

Automating the purchase of these products cuts down the time wasted by employees sending memos or awaiting approval for purchases. It has been calculated that this can reduce the cost of the buying process by as much as 95 per cent. Non-strategic purchases, such as pens and paper clips, appear trivial until we consider the recent IBM study that shows the average large corporation spends an estimated $160 million (£100 million or €155 million) a year on merchandise not related to production. The ability the Internet provides to easily seek out and compare sellers and prices anywhere in the world may bring down prices even for key pieces of inventory.

Many opportunities are soon to open up for supplying services to European governments. Most central government IT units are now looking to change to an IT-based strategy, ensuring that government purchasing (which, for example, accounts for four per cent of all UK goods and services) is fully electronic.

Manufacturers also issue far more purchase orders for maintenance consumables, computer equipment, office supplies, software, advertising, travel and entertainment than for raw materials. IT companies are now providing systems which manage purchases of such non-production goods and services centrally for which the main incentive to businesses are the attractive discounts on bulk purchasing. There would therefore seem to be many opportunities for small firms to take advantage of the Net to provide fast, efficient and competitively priced non-strategic goods direct to large organisations.

ELECTRONIC DATA INTERCHANGE

Electronic data interchange systems (EDI) technology enables suppliers to view stock levels, send contracts and receive and pay invoices electronically. Until recently only large firms have been able to afford EDI systems, but now that EDI is available over the Internet small firms can enjoy the profitable efficiency EDI can provide.

The aforementioned global reach and flexibility make it possible to extend electronic-trading capabilities to an expanding choice of new partners. The free access that the Internet provides allows both buyers and suppliers to benefit from lower costs. As the large companies explore the Internet more seriously, they may increase the number of transaction partners with whom they conduct EDI and electronic funds transfer (EFT), without any lengthy and costly set-up procedures, by offering a simple web interface.

Those set-up requirements, which involve agreeing on information needs, business procedures and technical arrangements, are repeated every time an organisation implements computer-to-computer EDI or EFT with a new transaction partner. Computer-to-computer EDI has long been the province of intranets and value-added networks (VANs), but the Internet makes possible interactive EDI in which suppliers engage in "spontaneous electronic commerce" by making order forms available over the Web. That information can then be converted into a standard protocol for EDI using the supplier's translation software.

EPOS

Many of the major European supermarket chains have recently decided to end their loyalty card schemes. This is partly because recent surveys have revealed that 90 per cent of their customers said that very few pieces of the unsolicited mail they received (as a consequence of the personal purchase details recorded on the cards) were of relevance to them. Most large companies are now starting to use other analytical software tools. However, most will continue to use electronic point-of-sale (EPOS) systems to analyse customer behaviour.

This trend brings into question the practice of collecting huge databases of customer information and the need for customers' names and addresses to personalise direct marketing. An alternative to loyalty schemes would be simple behavioural analysis conducted through analysing hits and requests on your company web pages.

At present, it is the innovative companies that are using EPOS to conduct analytical customer relationship management, as creative uses of analytic customer and marketing applications are paying dividends, but soon it will become standard practice both for consumer-to-business and business-to-business commerce. Using EPOS systems at your physical point-of-sale, in conjunction with your virtual web site point-of-sale, may give you the most accurate information from which to construct your customer profiles for target marketing.

INTERNET SUPPLY CHAIN

More and more large companies are encouraging their small suppliers to become part of an electronic supply chain — the route products take from production to retailers' shelves. Internet transmission reliability will soon be a solvable problem and, as for security, the Internet may be even safer than VANs because people are sensitised to its vulnerability. Being a VAN does not mean it is necessarily secure — it just means there are fewer people on it. People with legitimate access to the network can pose security risks as well.

For companies already present on the Internet, and those companies considering going online, there is also the appeal of being able to transmit key business documents over the same high-speed network they are using for e-mail, research and marketing, provided those networks are secure. But perhaps the most compelling reason to prefer the Internet to a VAN is cost. While security and reliability should be the most important considerations when comparing the two types of networks, the Net is less expensive by a factor of one-tenth, compared to the set-up cost of private in-house networks.[1]

The advent of extranet-enabling technologies such as eXtensible Markup Language (XML) is increasing the take-up of e-commerce with business partners over the Internet (see Chapter 5, The Future of Internet Commerce: XML). Manufacturers have been quick to seize on the potential of e-commerce. According to Forrester Research, 38 per cent of all world-wide business-to-business transactions will be conducted over the Web during 1999.[2]

The Web is starting to alter the dynamics of the supply chain, opening up possibilities for electronic trading with smaller suppliers, and also with customers. Over the next few years, distributors and retailers could find their business eroded as manufacturers move towards cutting out the middleman. The National Computing Centre (NCC) has estimated that the cost of receiving information via EDI systems is around 20 per cent of the cost of equivalent paper-based methods.

By building *extranets* (an intranet that includes suppliers), or private web systems, with ordering, billing and order tracking systems, manufacturers are making it possible to move information around the supply chain at a lower cost. To use the e-commerce system available on an extranet, all the supplier needs is a PC, browser, modem and Internet account.

> "Business-to-business is where most of the money is at the moment, although business-to-consumer e-commerce is rapidly growing. Businesses tend to be more aligned with the Internet, and there are also economies of scale" (Piers Hogarth-Scott, Director of Web Consultancy for Bluberry New Media, 1998).[3]

It is the influence of the Internet that is revolutionising supply chains. Firms can go online to gather information that enables them to provide products and services more quickly to the correct location without unnecessary build-up of stocks. Firms can now also monitor service levels by checking the efficiency of the supply chain. For example, the efficiency of haulage contractors can be monitored to determine whether they are delivering products to depots and customers on time.

INTERNET-BASED PROJECT MANAGEMENT

We have already witnessed many Internet solutions exploited by the service and manufacturing industries, but other less likely industries may soon benefit from Internet applications. For example, the construction industry has been guilty in the past of inefficiency, cost overruns and late delivery. However, it may soon take advantage of the Internet's flexibility, and through collaborative engineering improve its efficiency through Internet-based project management.

Architectural engineering and construction (AEC) software providers now offer construction project handlers Internet-based project management tools. Rather than Gantt chart-based projects, project-specific web sites are now available to engineers, subcontractors and those involved in a building project. Other products provide digital site photography or web-based meeting rooms in which project members can meet to review project plans or CAD (computer-aided design) drawings.

This method of working will aid JIT (just-in-time) building processes as contractors can now bring large pre-built sections to site just as they are needed. Building JIT partnerships with suppliers and customers saves significant amounts of operating capital, provides fast access to reliable data, reduces stock, requires less inventory and allows the orders cycle to be processed faster and more efficiently.

The construction industry is an excellent example of how companies involved in development projects of any kind can improve their efficiency through Internet-based project management

COMMERCIAL PORTAL WEB SITES

Industrial web portals, or so-called "enterprise portals", are predicted to cause a paradigm shift within the manufacturing industry. Companies such as SAP (www.mysap.com) are now starting to offer web portals to provide operating resources management (ORM) software and business-to-business services to other businesses. The information is delivered through a standard web browser, which provides access to other sites and services. PeopleSoft has similar ambitions for its PSBN Merchant programme.

The intention of business-to-business portal sites such as these is to provide advice, products or services that can assist manufacturers through every stage of the value chain. Other companies are providing facilities and solutions such as enterprise resource planning (ERP) software. JBA promises a series of different industry-specific news portals, including just-food.com (www.just-food.com). More and more companies are providing industry-specific news portals. For example, CAD supplier PTC's InPart portal has been expanded to include whatever electronic component data is required by their online customers. This is an area of business-to-business e-commerce that is guaranteed to increase in the future.

INDUSTRY-SPECIFIC RESOURCE WEB SITES

By putting your product database on the Web you enable your customers to know any of your latest product specifications immediately. The Web has allowed firms, such as electronics manufacturers, to reach a much broader audience than it could before, especially engineers overseas. Also, by making information about your components easier to come by, product designers will be more likely to specify your products over your competitor's (see Chapter 6, Case Studies: *Kanda Systems Ltd.*).

Product data books, catalogues and CD-ROMs cannot always reach an entire target audience (e.g. approximately one million engineers incorporate electronic components into their products), but the Web has given companies a ready-made delivery system. However, market research indicates that if people are required to spend more than three minutes to find information from a web site, they tend not to use it. Thus keeping a web search of a large database to less than three minutes is a challenge, but it may be imperative.

The service industry is also starting to witness the provision of industry-specific web sites offering advice, facilities and alternative channels to market. For example, Autolocate (www. autolo-cate.co.uk) is a company that provides Internet services for car dealers. It requires 750 car dealers to subscribe to its online service to break even. At £99 (€149) a month, a dealer has to sell one or two cars a year through this new marketing channel for it to have paid for itself.

It is predicted that there will soon be a number of motoring channels representing most areas of Europe on the Net, offering services such as business-to-consumer and business-to-business car-buying services. They will probably offer more than just basic car supply. They will offer analysis of warranties and insurance, traffic news, information on breakdown and recovery services and car reviews, as well as offering the retailer services in building and managing a motoring web site.

Industry-specific resource web sites, portal sites and even ISPs are likely to become an integral facet of business-to-business e-commerce over the next few years.

NETWORK INTEGRATION

A model of the future may be one where businesses use the Internet to send information to everyone else but only certain *types* of information. The Internet would be the place where everyone does research, disseminates information and does their marketing; then they switch off to another network to do their business transactions. In the future, companies may well be using the entire infrastructure of the information highway, not the Internet alone. They may have the choice of the appropriate network for the appropriate task.

GLOBAL NETWORKS

There may be a need to move toward a future paradigm where there is one globally integrated virtual network. Such that, if a company is conducting commercial transactions on the Internet, it may gateway to the VANs, the VANs can gateway to another company, and the whole thing is transparent to the various business entities. While Internet access will become universal, companies may use it only to augment their own private networks. But even such restricted usage may be critical, especially as countries in Eastern Europe, the Far East and other underdeveloped areas embrace, and are embraced by, global commerce.

Some of the most sophisticated web-based "marketspaces" are being developed in countries that have previously lacked the resources to develop a modern communications infrastructure. For example, in China, the China Internet Company is building a network among 40 different Chinese cities that will use the Web as a network to exchange product information, pricing, e-mail, relevant import/export regulations and an online translation service. Global integration will be the future of Internet commerce and, consequently, it will require new export controls, export duties and new international licensing laws and trading agreements.[4] As for the future of Internet commerce, it is important that small firms are aware of the opportunities for global business-to-business trading.

TRANSLATION

Currently, 80 per cent of the content on the Web is in English and 60 per cent is still American in content. However, American companies find it difficult to recognise that Europe is a mix of different cultures that require content developed for each nationality not just a translated version of a web site. There will inevitably be a future demand from European companies for Internet solution providers as well as translation services. Adding major European languages, such as French and German, or world languages such as Spanish or English, to your site, or providing a full language-specific version of your site, could see a rise in visitors and online sales.

Translation rates are relatively inexpensive. However, small firms are only just coming to terms with the concept and cost of web sites and are reluctant to pay again to have them translated. If the extra expense is a concern it should be remembered that you do not have to translate an entire site. A brief message in different languages may uncover a lot of new markets. There are automatic free online translators such as Systran (www.crabbe-gen-store. com/systran.htm) that offer a basic translation solution. Developing a language-specific or multilingual site will cost approximately 10 to 20 per cent more than an English-only site. At approximately £10 for 100 words, European languages are the least expensive.

VENTURE CAPITAL

Money for Internet-related businesses is now being made available to entrepreneurs in Europe as venture capitalists and investment companies such as Apax provide seed capital as they become more aware of the opportunities for e-commerce. Another early investor, the investment group Durlacher, has stakes in many UK Internet companies planning flotation. Others include Bernard Arnault, the French business tycoon who has recently set up Europ@Web and invested in 20 European start-ups.

The big European banks such as Deutsche Bank are all now eager to invest in Internet start-ups. Media tycoon Rupert Murdoch has also got involved with funding new Internet-based firms through Epartners. Epartners and Softbank have formed a joint fund, e-Ventures, that has an estimated £32 million (€48 million) to spend. Other Internet-related investment companies include E*Trade and Cyberspace forum Geocities.

Throughout Europe many companies are becoming increasingly interested in investing in firms committed to e-commerce. Just as some companies are more committed to e-commerce than others, some countries are investing more in the high-tech future.

Countries such as Ireland are now ready for phase two of their Internet commerce-related high-tech industry growth. There are already hundreds of existing Irish-owned Internet-related firms which are attracting many venture capitalists. In the last three years alone, 12 Irish, UK and US venture firms have located in Ireland.

Presently, the economic climate could not be better for those small companies requiring financial assistance to build an Internet presence. For most small firms it is definitely worthwhile considering outside investment if seed capital is required.

BUSINESS CONSULTANCY

The Internet has not just provided another channel through which companies can market their goods and services. With any new industry comes the opportunity for other businesses to provide complementary or support products and services. Consultancy was the first industry to grow out of companies' demand for guidance concerning e-commerce and online marketing. Since then there has been a steadily increasing demand from small businesses for consultancy, web building, Internet-solutions, etc.

As the largest of consultancies and solution providers price themselves outside the budget of most small businesses, there are opportunities for firms with the relevant skills to provide smaller companies with the required structure to conduct Internet commerce successfully.

Lime Internet Solutions (www.limeonline.co.uk) is an example of a new and dynamic company with a varied and proven skills base in the computing solutions arena. It offers services ranging from fixed price hardware, consultancy, web design, hosting, marketing, project management and e-commerce packages. We are likely to witness other companies following this model of an Internet-solutions provider as demand from the small business sector grows in the new millennium.

References

[1] Frost, A. & Norris, M. *Exploiting the Internet: Understanding and Exploiting an Investment in the Internet* (John Wiley & Sons: UK) 1997, p. 2

[2] *Computing*, 8 October 1998, p. 52

[3] *PC Weekly*, 24 October 1998, p. 38

[4] www.dti.gov.uk/export.control.

5

THE FUTURE OF INTERNET COMMERCE

"What are the business processes that are important? It's unlikely that the Net is now, but it may well be in the future"
(Peter Nolan, Head of IT Vision Centre, 1998).[1]

Direct pay-per-view Internet access, Internet TV, and the increasing amount of European schools with Internet access, will provide
future businesses with a generation of highly computer literate
and Internet-familiar potential customers. They are likely to grow-
up into a highly technologically-advanced environment without
the doubts and suspicions most consumers presently have regarding technology and the Internet. This generation is likely to
be the one that gives the World Wide Web its momentum. As this
audience is increased it may provide a much larger cross-section
of potential customers, creating a wider target market for online
merchants.

"The next big break through will be mass market acceptance
of the Web and by 2003 over 50 million will be using it" (John
McFarlane, President of Solaris Software, 1998).[2]

Over time, the next generation of Internet shoppers may not be so
reticent to order products and services online due to the inevitable
savings to be made. Online shopping will not replace every aspect
of consumer behaviour. However, it will make a significant difference. The principal reason for customers to shop offline may be
pleasure. Where cost and convenience are less important than

being made to feel cosseted, admired or that little bit special, the pleasure principle may still demand a trip to favourite shops.[3]

Our need for social interaction will preserve retail outlets, which will either cater for customer needs to be seen shopping or to provide emergency stock and "disposables" such as toilet paper and cigarettes etc. Potentially, most other products may be bought over the Internet. If this is to be the future, most of the hindrances to setting up a business will no longer exist. The need for property, rent, and staff will be virtually removed. If a company uses a break-even order level before ordering stock or work as an intermediary for larger producers, stock holding will also be unnecessary. In theory, all a business will require is a computer, modem and telephone line.

Telecommunications companies, such as British Telecom (BT), may soon devastate the future of the Internet service provider industry. BT has recently announced its intention to provide customers with simple and direct access to the Internet without the need to subscribe to a service provider. Prices for this service may be the same as BT's standard local call rates and will appear on a customer's phone bill. The new pay-per-view service is designed to establish BT as a dominant European company in web access provision since this new service will dispense with the commitment customers make to an ISP.[4]

INTERNET SERVICE PROVISION

In the future, simple Internet service provision will become a commodity, as is demonstrated by the increasing amount of free consumer-orientated Internet services providers. At present, only 35 per cent of European Internet users use a free-access service, but 90 per cent of users are predicted to use them by 2002.[6] Some ISPs are now touting themselves as value-added service providers who can construct and host an e-commerce solution for their customers.

One advantage of siding with a host service provider is that a company may be able to take advantage of the interfaces to credit card clearing services. This will enable a customer's credit-worthiness to be verified online so that their order can be confirmed while they are still connected to the server. Services such as these will be important to online traders regardless of whether e-commerce is conducted through a PC interface with customers or other rival technologies.

MOBILES

The mobile phones and multimedia devices of the future will have large screens, built-in cameras, listening devices and be able to receive and transmit TV and video pictures. They will be capable of being used anywhere in the world and the new networks on which they will operate will be designed never to lose a call. The introduction of third-generation (3G) digital mobile phones and devices will eventually allow users to access e-mail, Internet sites, corporate e-mail and even conduct video-conferencing through easy-to-use products capable of delivering CD-quality music, Internet TV and radio. The technology will make mobile phone Internet access as fast as a high-speed digital ISDN line without cables or phone sockets.

However, the standard mobile network on which these 3G mobiles will be used is far from certain. GSM (Global System of Mobile Communications), which replaced analogue systems primarily for voice calls, is now the predominant standard in Europe, Asia and Australasia. Data is currently sent almost six times slower than a conventional modem, making Internet access slow and expensive. Though GSM networks will continue to be used for voice after the new mobile devices are introduced, the following three networks are set to become the dominant mobile telecommunications systems in the future:

- GPRS (General Packet Radio Service) can operate on existing GSM digital mobile phone networks but handle data at twice the speed of a standard modem. GPRS is a packet-switched technology designed to extend an Internet connection across the GSM network to a PC. GPRS data is sent in "packets" to the Internet provider but is only used when it needs a packet to be sent or received thus making Internet access faster.

- UMTS (Universal Mobile Telecommunications Service) is the first network to be designed specifically to carry voice and data reliably. It uses a different portion of the radio spectrum to GSM and is based on an agreed worldwide standard.

- HSCSD (High-Speed Circuit Switched Data) employs a new channel-coding scheme that increases the transmission rate of each time slot and allows for multiple time slots to be combined into a single channel. Also, because it is circuit-switched, it offers guaranteed bandwidth.

GSM may have been the technology that put digital mobile telephony on the world map but one of these new wireless data technologies will be necessary to conduct uninterruptible and secure e-commerce in the future.

OTHER UTILITIES

Other Internet-compatible multimedia devices will probably become commonplace. Already, there are permanent stand-alone information booths and terminals to be found through many major European cities. There are also plans to set-up Internet-linked multimedia kiosks at public meeting places, such as bus stops, throughout Europe. These "i-plus" kiosks consist of a PC with a touch-screen, a credit card reader and printer contained in a steel case, which is linked to a central server via ISDN. Information will be delivered through a series of branded channels giving details of tickets, local bus routes, travel news and tourist information. In the future these terminals and interactive screens will be more numerous and will provide the whole spectrum of Internet and TV-related services.

FUTURE INNOVATIONS

Most experts confidently predict that within only a few years' time we will be using computers the size of cigarette packets that are capable of storing as much data as 350 PCs by exploiting the storage properties of new metal alloys. Data storage technology will be so efficient that thousands of gigabytes of data will be stored on to devices the size of a credit card. These "three-dimensional memory systems" (3Ds) will provide the highest circuit density ever achieved. This, and other innovations, is likely to bring a revolution in computer design do away with conventional hard disk drives.

The technology will be scalable, either up or down, so that even the smallest of devices will be capable of handling memory capacity of hundreds of gigabytes. Future PC processors and memories will probably be joined as a single unit with minimal power consumption and minimal production costs. Because innovations such as these can be applied beyond PCs, TVs and digital cameras, future multimedia devices are likely to be similar in size to slim cards with almost limitless storage capacity.

BANDWIDTH

The volume of Internet traffic doubles every 100 days as more people come online. This traffic eats up the bandwidth (the measure of how data flows) of its data network. To increase bandwidth, telecos use huge fibre-optic cable global networks. These fibre-optic cables transmit digital data using light, which shift huge amounts of data over vast distances relatively cheaply. The science of using particles of light to shift data and use light to switch packets of data along networks is known as "photonics".

New photonic technologies, such as wave division multiplexing (WDM), are expected to increase bandwidth. WDM allows the light travelling down a single-fibre cable to be split into many different colours, each colour able to act like a single cable, and usually multiplying capacity by 40. It is now possible to put many of the components for WDM on a single silicon chip using Active Silicon Optical Circuits (ASOC) technology, making it possible to form complex optical circuits. Each circuit consists of a number of interconnected basic optical components, such as transmitters; receivers, switches and routers on low-cost silicon devices for the growing optical transmission market.

It is hoped that technologies such as these will soon provide fast bandwidth across all platforms and allow quicker and more reliable digital access in the near future.

XML

Over the next few years we will witness the increasing use of XML (eXtensible Markup Language) alongside the current Internet language HTML. Mainly to improve the efficiency of searches over the Internet, XML will simplify communications between different systems and speed up the retrieval of data contained within web pages.

XML enables the manipulation of platform-independent data. It can "tag" any kind of data, allowing machines to understand what kind of data it contains. Content therefore becomes more accessible to different software and less dependent on specific output devices. Internet users will achieve more meaningful results with fewer false hits.

For companies expanding into e-commerce, XML will provide low-cost ways to exchange purchase orders and other business documents seamlessly over the Internet. In the near future, small businesses will be able to create complex order forms and catalogues and use XML for Internet EDI applications at much lower cost.

XML documents are text-based so they can be distributed easily over the Internet; they are readable so all you need is a text editor to edit them. Microsoft's *Internet Explorer* 5.0 supports XML, and it also has the support of all other sectors of the information technology industry, so it is likely to be taken up universally very quickly. The language will build on existing technology investments and extend many application functionalities. All commercial and consumer markets will use XML browsers within the next ten years.

INTERNET2

Microsoft may not be renowned as an innovative company, but it is always quick to respond to profitable IT sectors and trends. By following its lead you can usually tell which technologies are most likely to dominate in the future. Microsoft Research has recently been investing heavily in developing a new Internet network (Internet2), which they expect to be more efficient and reliable. Together with 150 universities and corporate partners IBM, Cisco, AT&T and 3Com, their aim is to develop a network that can move data at speeds up to 1,000 times faster than today's Internet.

Billions of dollars, euro and yen are being invested in Internet - related technologies from both the private and public sectors. Therefore, even if television-based media does dominate our lives in the future, the Internet is guaranteed to become a mass media in its own right, whether it exists alongside TV or integrated within it. Television-based advertising will remain the primary advertising medium for large organisations. The small business sector will therefore be supported more and more by Internet-based media in the future.

INTERNET-ENHANCED TV

"The boundary between what is a TV and what is a PC will be completely blurred" (Bill Gates, 1998).[5]

The Internet's main rival for future business-to-customer e-commerce will be interactive digital television (IDTV). IDTV provides a good model for e-commerce, where interactive cable links a digital television receiver to a broadcaster. IDTV viewers will receive broadcasts not only from television broadcasters but also from Coca-Cola, Visa and Barclays, etc. Any company with sufficient financial resources will hire capacity from the cable companies and set up an electronic shopping service by broadcasting straight to the home. IDTV will, for the foreseeable future, be the preferred medium of large market brands.

For example, Woolworths, who have traditionally sold low-glamour goods to the mass market and therefore do not have an ideal strategic fit for e-commerce, has ignored the Internet and its primarily middle-class web buyers. But now that interactive TV is available, Woolworths expects a huge customer response to their IDTV service. Other companies, such as Abbey National, Argos, Dixons, Manchester United, First Call, HSBC and Somerfield are expected to set up IDTV-based marketing campaigns.

IDTV provides Internet access with data being transmitted along with the TV signal, although both terrestrial and satellite TV need a phone line to provide the link from the user to the broadcaster. "Internet-enhanced TV" is transmitted by television broadcasting companies to normal domestic televisions, as well as home PCs equipped with a TV card, sound card and TV aerial or cable. Subscribers are provided with interactive multimedia TV or Internet access without having to tune in or download.

The new digital services will broadcast a binary signal that has to be decoded by a computer (a digital signal processor) at the receiving end before it can be turned into a picture on a screen. Digital broadcasting has many advantages. It uses less bandwidth per channel so more separate signals can be broadcast using the same spectrum (digital or satellite). All kinds of digital information, which was previously difficult or very time-consuming to acquire, will be made immediately available. Web content in particular can be broadcast and cached locally. Popular sites will become instantly available, rather than having to be downloaded slowly over a modem connection.

Currently, the main piece of equipment required to receive Internet TV is the set-top box. This device, together with a telephone line, can turn a domestic TV into an Internet machine with web browsing and e-mail capabilities. An infrared wireless keyboard is necessary to write to screen, or via the TV remote or telephone. It is Internet TV that may provide low-cost, high-speed net access for millions of people who would not otherwise use the Web. The future integration of favourite TV programmes, home entertainment and web sites all sharing the same delivery system and advertising medium, may well prove decisive in establishing e-commerce.

In the UK, Internet use has been growing by about 50 per cent a year, but from a tiny base. According to the consultancy Jupiter, in the UK alone 4.5 million British households should be online by the end of 1999. At the end of 1998 it was 3 million; the year before that it was 2 million. Compare that with the number of households with a television, approximately 26 million, and the Internet audience is still very small, especially when the demographics of that audience is taken into account.

According to British Interactive Broadcasting (BIB), more people in the UK have access to a TV set than a PC — almost 40 per cent of UK homes have a PC whereas 98 per cent have a TV. The difference in ratio between PC and TV owners is likely to be even greater in Europe than in the UK. Also, PCs are generally viewed by the public as hard to use, unreliable and uncomfortable, whereas TV is seen as reliable and simple to use.

Although the Internet audience is growing, it is only tapping into certain groups of the world's population. Global Interactive digital TV will not just increase the Internet audience, it will also access groups that today have not yet considered using the Internet. Digital TV will let large corporations and global brands tap a market of millions of consumers so far untouched by the Internet.

Almost all potential customers would prefer to shop using the remote control on their TV set than on their PC using the Internet. Also, unlike PCs, digital TV set-top boxes are supplied and installed free. Successful retailing on the Internet is likely to become limited to large Internet-related businesses or small businesses with the correct strategic fit for e-commerce. Most likely it will only be the large corporations that will be able to afford to advertise on TV-specific media and dominate this new channel to market.

It is likely to be these large brands that TV channels will want to be associated with. Also, companies can leverage their brands more effectively through television, because they do not have to compete with small net marketers. Reputable companies with a name to protect will prefer IDTV because it places them in an electronic version of the High Street, a commercial environment they understand. They will find that the interactive nature of IDTV makes charging simpler and identification of customers more straightforward.

The shoppers themselves will prefer IDTV because they will be able to shop with confidence. They will know they are dealing with the genuine company because they are receiving the broadcast. Trust will be built into this system. As for governments, they too prefer this medium. Monitoring, regulation and taxation of trade will be much easier. As proof of the future significance of IDTV, European broadcasting companies are soon to introduce e-commerce services, and Microsoft has already bought into this competitor technology.

Microsoft recently negotiated a number of business deals with cable television and optical fibre companies throughout Europe and the US worth an estimated $1 billion (€950 million). Since 1996, when Microsoft bought WebTV, the company has been working towards a future where hand-held devices and interactive TV will replace PCs as the most popular means of accessing the Internet. Many other companies are also convinced of the impact IDTV and other Internet/TV technologies will have.

The Management Consultancies Association (MCA), which includes Andersen Consulting, CSC, Ernst & Young and IBM Consulting, predicts that digital Internet-enhanced television will become the focus for future electronic sales and will leave PC-driven Internet access behind. It takes the view that PC access will no longer provide a large enough market to justify large retailers' investment in e-commerce.

But do not expect setting up in digital TV to be as simple as setting up on the Internet since you cannot simply transport your existing web site to the TV. There are huge barriers to entry into this new service area apart from the expense. You will have to spend time and money redesigning existing pages to suit TV, or start again from scratch. You will have to change your existing pages so they will be easier for non-PC literate users to read and navigate.

These changes will require reducing the amount of jargon and text used, using compatible colour palettes and graphic display formats, simplifying design for maximum televisual impact, along with eliminating scroll bars and adapting the page sizes as well as spreading information across multiple pages and providing navigation for a remote control. Banner adverts and links to other Internet sites may also have to be removed. Therefore, only businesses that can identify a huge benefit in IDTV should undertake these changes. This new technology will produce a different customer profile and will therefore require efficient and flexible back-end business structures to support this new channel to market.

For the next few years at least, these alternative technologies will be the preferred medium for the large corporations. For smaller companies, with the correct strategic fit, the Internet will remain the most cost-effective advertising medium for many years to come.

References

[1] *Computing*, 17 September 1998, p. 20

[2] *Sunday Times*, "Getting Wired: Computing for Small and Medium-Sized Firms", 19 October 1997, p. 2

[3] *PC Guide Magazine*, August, 1998, p. 28

[4] *Internet Works* Magazine, Issue 9, August, 1998, p. 9

[6] *Business Lunch*, BBC 2, 13 April 1999

[5] Gates, B., *PC Advisor Magazine*, February, 1998, p. 70.

6

CASE STUDIES

The purpose of using actual case studies is to illustrate which
businesses have the correct strategic fit for e-commerce. The following list of small businesses represents a wide spectrum of
commerce: retail, service, manufacturing, entertainment and leisure sectors. Using the *Strategic Fit Matrix* (page 82), we can predict or confirm whether each company should be successful online.

The ten case studies are:

1. Body Basics

2. Catapult 100% Vinyl

3. eBid

4. Kanda Systems Limited

5. Mansfield Motors

6. North East Militaria & Surplus

7. Pub Paraphernalia

8. Strange Fruits

9. The Graphics Company

10. Trophy Miniatures of Wales.

BODY BASICS

Body Basics is a clothes shop run by the owner and employs one full-time, and two part-time, sales advisors. It was established in 1986. The shop specialises in exclusive designer wear for women but also sells various accessories including designer jewellery and domestic appliances. The target market sectors are socio-economic groups A, B, C1. The unique selling point of the business is its limited edition designer clothing and the individual customer service it can provide. Most customers learn of the business through advertising in quality magazines or word-of-mouth.

The customer profile for this particular business would suggest that an Internet presence for the business would be extraneous to its needs. Current customers are very unlikely to use any Internet facilities and potential customers are unlikely to be contacted or attracted to the business through Internet marketing. As these products may not be available to people living in areas without exclusive designer-label retail outlets, there may be an opportunity to sell through a combination of mail order and e-commerce in the future, provided access to the Internet becomes considerably more wide-spread.

CATAPULT 100% VINYL

Catapult 100% Vinyl (www.catapult.co.uk) is a specialist dance-music shop owned by two partners who employ six specialist sales staff. Catapult opened in 1994 as a standard retail outlet and mail order business advertising in the national music press. The shop provides state-of-the-art equipment for customers to hear records before purchase and provides listening facilities for those ordering by phone.

In 1995 it set up a web site virtual shop. It now conducts a fifth of its total sales through the web site, and encourages electronic credit card transactions. The site consists of more than 50 pages of music and merchandise and has a search engine facility plus an online retail service comparable with anything in the High Street. Two members of staff spend one day a week fully updating the online store. The site is also updated daily with new releases and pre-release stock by six specialist buyers.

PLATE 6.1: CATAPULT 100% VINYL

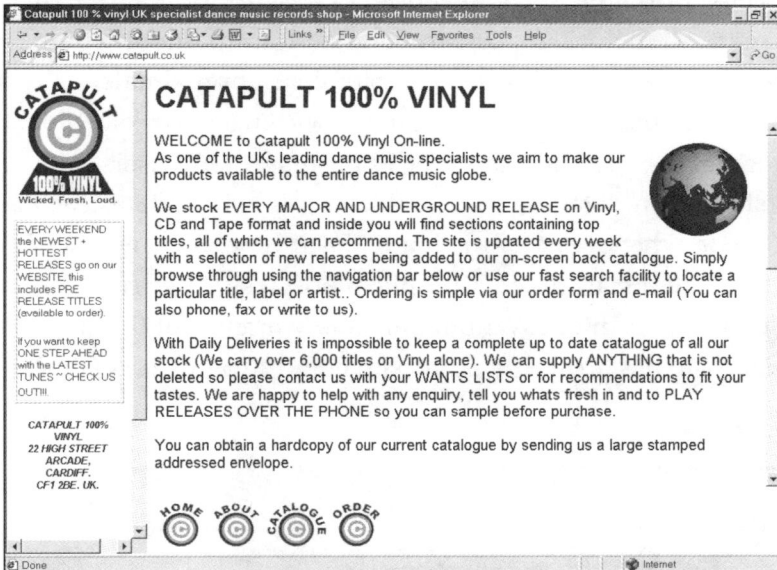

The success of this venture has been consolidated by the development of the virtual shop on the company's web site. The company's successful Internet commerce seems to be due to the specialisation of the company and by allowing their potential customers to browse the virtual store in their own time. In general, the facility to browse at the user's convenience appears to be a major influence on successful Internet commerce. Specialisation and a browsing facility seem to be common denominators in any successful web site presence.

The Internet-user's psychological, socio-economic, and demographic profiles fit the outline of this company's target market perfectly. In all, this particular business appears to be an excellent example of the kind of enterprise that can benefit fullest from e-commerce.

EBID

eBid (www.ebid.com) is one of the latest editions to the fast growing sector of online auctions. eBid is the work of a single owner-manager. All the design, construction and programming of the entire site was done in-house. The site cost approximately £10,000 (€15,500) to build and was constructed within six weeks. eBid's target market are the UK and other English-speaking users. The eBid web site uses a database system that stores and updates each auction's data whenever a bid is made. Each new eBid member is offered a £2 (€3) starting credit while eBid takes 2 per cent commission on each sale made. Within only a few months of trading eBid's membership has grown by approximately 100 new users per day.

PLATE 6.2: EBID

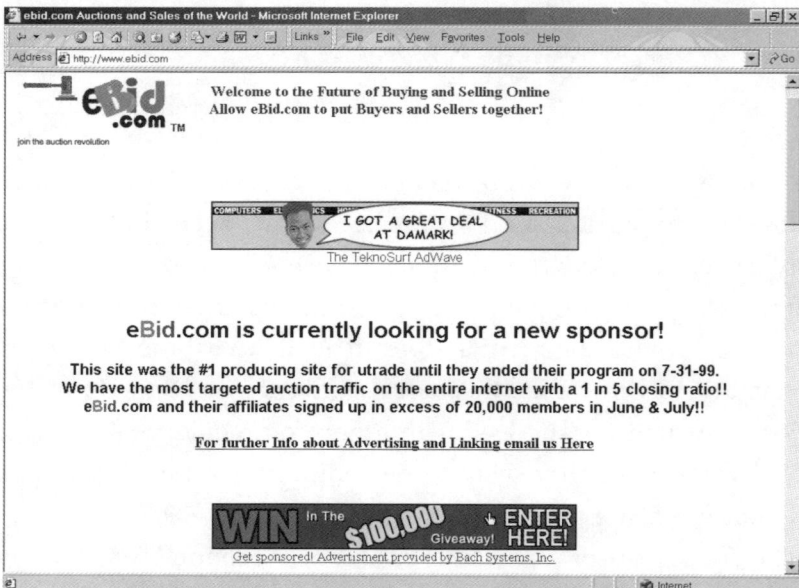

eBid must establish itself as a top UK brand within this sector to compete as this online market sector is already well established. As with most online industries, unless a small business is early to establish itself in a market sector it will have to create a niche on-line market for itself. It is predicted that auctions will be very popular in the near future when the Internet is integrated more fully into a television-based format and people can access auctions on their living room TV.

KANDA SYSTEMS LIMITED

Kanda Systems Limited (www.Kanda.com), founded in 1994, is an independent company run by two former college lecturers. The company specialises in assisting organisations with the rapid development of applications for micro-electronics. Kanda's equipment helps engineers work on the silicon chips that control various electronic devices. Engineers, particularly in the computer and electronics industries, use the Internet to research completed designs that can be adapted for their own specific purpose and develop or adapt chip designs or acquire the necessary tools for the job.

Since the firm has been trading on the Internet it has grown from a two-man firm operating from a shed to a leading company in its field world-wide, employing 32 staff. It is set to turn over £1.9 million (€2.9 million) by the end of 1999 and 95 per cent of the firm's sales are now exported. The result is a comprehensive range of development tools, training programmes and associated products backed by a support team focused on addressing the needs of the customer at all levels of technical ability. The company's dedicated manufacturing research and development facility enables it to take products from the drawing board to delivery in the shortest time possible.

PLATE 6.3: KANDA SYSTEMS LIMITED

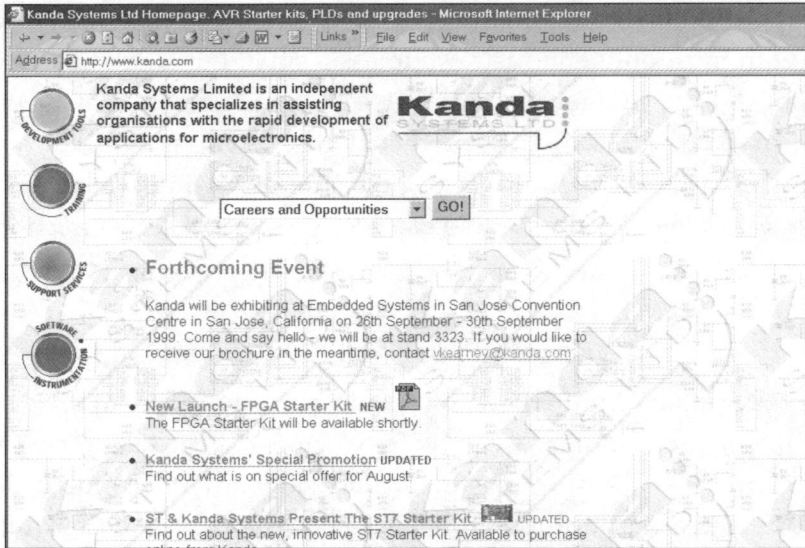

In addition, the company will also undertake bespoke programming and design consultancy projects on behalf of its customers. In instances where a customer has a specific requirement that they are unable to fulfil, Kanda will endeavour to procure a suitable product or, if necessary, submit a proposal to design one. Users can also take advantage of Kanda's comprehensive range of complete training packages such as starter kits, which makes it possible for even the smallest of developers to extend its portfolio of skills and services into an area previously prohibited by cost.

Kanda Systems Ltd. is an excellent example of how a small business, providing a specialised, genuinely useful product which is difficult to acquire elsewhere, to a niche market, can be extremely successful online. Kanda proves that by establishing a buyer-seller relationship through providing information about their products, a small firm can achieve consistent, repeat orders. Kanda also has the dependable back-end structures in place. It uses a parcel courier delivery service and its products are available internationally through major distributors and catalogue-based organisations to cope with any potential demand. This case study also illustrates the potential for small firms to be successful online by supplying other firms.

MANSFIELD MOTORS

Mansfield Motors (www.mansfield-motors.com) is an owner-manager small business that now specialises in Land Rover spares. In the 12 months since first advertising from its web site, the company has gained £150,000 (€232,500) in extra business. This increase in trade has already transformed the company from a small local garage into a global business employing eight staff.

PLATE 6.4: MANSFIELD MOTORS

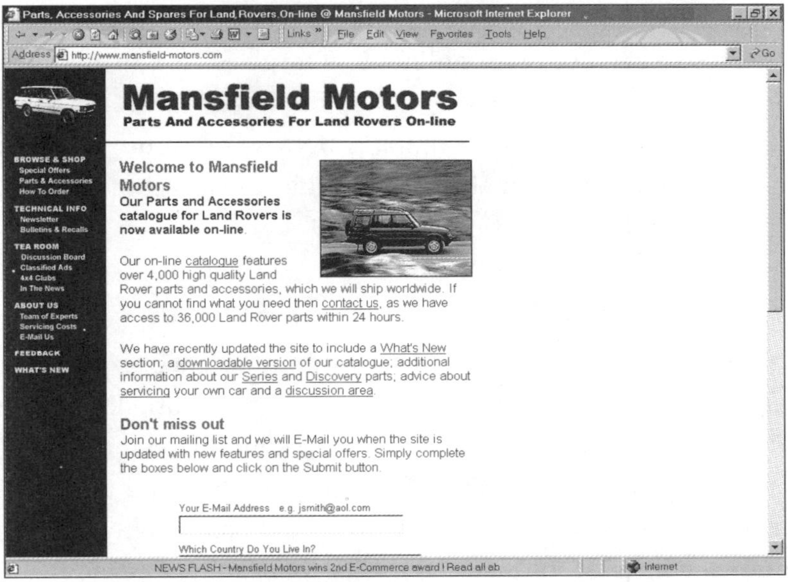

In only a year, from being a non-export business, it now exports 70 per cent of its parts abroad, all due to its Internet-related enquiries. As is evident from other successful Internet-based businesses, specialisation has been the key element in this company's success. Because this company can offer Land Rover enthusiasts specialised information, and spare parts at cheaper prices, it has developed its workshop trade globally. Currently 20 per cent of its orders are from Europe and the Middle East.

Since the company started trading online, its web site has been developed to create a user-friendly and knowledgeable environment that the owner believes helps to create customer trust. The web site also has value-added features, such as customer feedback, discussion and advice areas. It also attempts to create its own one-to-one customer relationships through virtual customer community creation schemes such as its Land Rover Club membership scheme.

This web site is an excellent example of how a small company with the correct strategic fit for e-commerce can overcome geographic and market barriers through trading over the Internet. This business follows nearly all the prerequisites necessary for businesses to be successful online. It is targeted at a niche market through a strong brand name, uses added-value features to help encourage customer relationships, offers a premium value-for-money service and is capable of handling most technical and logistical demands.

NORTH EAST MILITARIA & SURPLUS

North East Militaria & Surplus (www.btinternet.com/~ne.mas/) is a sole trader business, not employing any staff, that started trading in 1994. The shop sells military collectables and surplus army equipment and clothing. The company has had an Internet presence since 1995. The company web site has quickly grown to account for at least 10 per cent of its total annual turnover. Recently, due to the increasing popularity of auction sites, the company has begun to exploit the Net audience's interest in collectables through the online bidding sites such as eBid (see Case Studies: eBid). The company accepts all major credit cards and online orders, including customer credit card details, by e-mail.

PLATE 6.5: NORTH EAST MILITARIA & SURPLUS

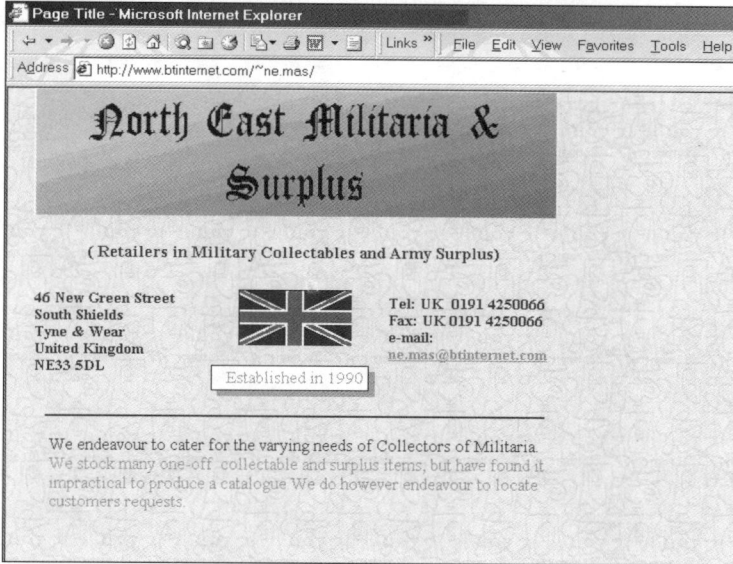

This case study is an example of how a micro business can diversify and expand its potential customer base to a global audience. The site was built in-house (using Microsoft *Publisher*) and has none of the cosmetic add-ons or plug-ins of a commercially built site. This has reduced the set-up and maintenance costs and the site has already achieved an excellent cost/profit margin which looks set to improve even more in the future.

PUB PARAPHERNALIA

Pub Paraphernalia (www.pub-paraphernalia.com) was established in 1980. The business is a limited company and employs four full-time staff in its warehouse, using outside packers for making up many of its products. A freelance designer, which the company keeps on a monthly retainer, develops the site on an ongoing basis. The site was developed to generate direct retail sales from the public but, to date, the total volume of business has not produced the impact that was hoped. However, several large customers found out about the company via Pub Paraphernalia's web site.

PLATE 6.6: PUB PARAPHERNALIA

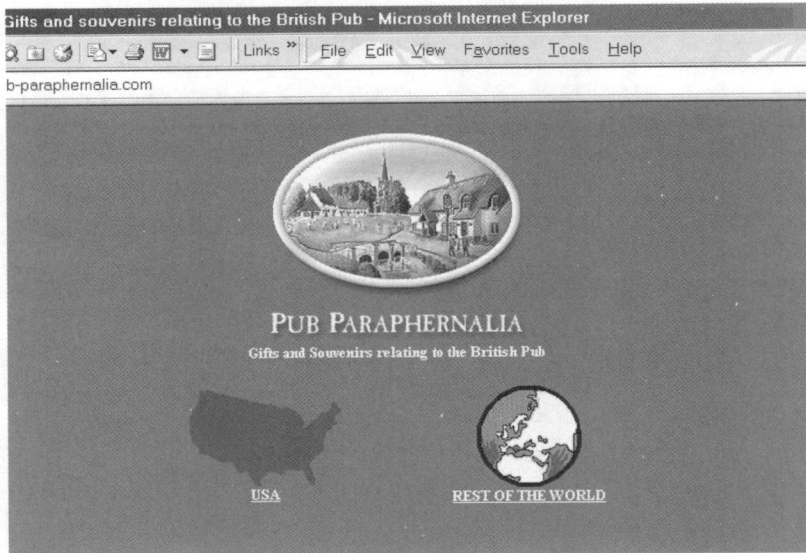

The company's web site is attracting an ever-increasing number of visitors each day; on average it now receives over 100 separate enquiries daily and the company expects this number to continue to increase. The company has reached its next stage of web site development and is now concentrating on broadening its scope and promoting it more extensively. This promotional plan includes making the site a much more dynamic and user-friendly environment. The company also intends to establish reciprocal links with compatible partners in the near future. The company's online success is due in part to its niche appeal to the large American and Japanese Internet audiences that are intrigued by the British pub.

STRANGE FRUITS

Strange Fruits manufacture and bottle essential aromatherapy oils and provide aromatherapy and reflexology services for women. It is a single owner-manager company that has been trading since 1990 from the owner's home. Apart from advertising in the standard telephone directories the company also advertises in specialist health shops.

Given that the company produces a relatively specialised product there may well be an opportunity to develop a web presence for Internet commerce. Aromatherapy oils would seem to fit the profile of the kind of specialist product that small producers are most successful in selling over the Internet. Also, research seems to suggest the typical Internet shopper tends to buy products over the Net that they can browse over, which they may not be so inclined to do (or may not have the time to do) when High Street shopping. Male shoppers may also appreciate the anonymous ordering system the Net provides. The main case against the expense of the company developing a web site would be the male-dominated profile of Internet users. There may, however, exist a profitable niche market, as there are already many similar producers online.

THE GRAPHICS COMPANY

The Graphics Company (www.the-graphics.co.uk) is a small design company specialising in graphic design and print management for voluntary and private sector organisations. The company is a co-operative of five people that has been trading for over nine years. The company believes that having a co-operative structure makes them more cost-effective due to less management and administrative overheads. Also, being able to communicate directly to the design team allows for a more personalised and efficient way of doing business.

PLATE 6.7: THE GRAPHICS COMPANY

Currently, the company has not yet conducted sales over the Internet but is hoping to use its Internet presence to broaden the company's appeal geographically, as it has previously concentrated on a local client base. The expansion of web site-based commerce in the near future should create an increasing demand for graphics-enhanced channels to market. However, at present the co-op is one of the many organisations that only use their Internet presence as part of their overall marketing mix and use their web site to provide information and encourage enquiries (see Chapter 3, Small Business Opportunities on the Internet: Graphic Art).

TROPHY MINIATURES OF WALES

Trophy Miniatures of Wales (www.btinternet.com/~trophy-swec/tropsud.htm) are makers of fine traditional toy soldiers. The company manufactures a selection of over 3,000 items. The specialist company was developed by one owner-manager. He creates, by hand, detailed miniatures based on traditional toy soldiers. Despite growing demand for trophy models, the standards are still the very highest. Each model is cast in premium quality white metal and individually hand-finished before the process of hand painting begins. These small works of art are produced in limited quantities.

PLATE 6.8: TROPHY MINIATURES OF WALES

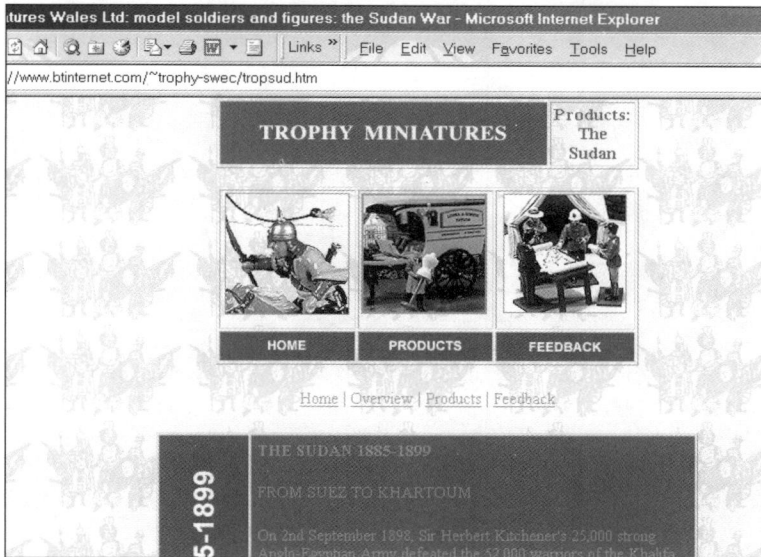

This company now trades on the Internet through a project initiated by the Electronic Commerce Innovation Centre, University of Wales, Cardiff. As a manufacturer producing a specialist product to a niche market, with a male orientation, it fits the profile of a business well suited to e-commerce. This business represents an excellent example of how a small company might exploit e-commerce if it has the correct strategic fit for the Internet.

STRATEGIC FIT MATRIX (0 = POOR STRATEGIC FIT; ½ = PARTIAL STRATEGIC FIT; 1 = GOOD STRATEGIC FIT)

Checklist	Body Basics	Catapult 100% Vinyl	eBid	Kanda Systems	Mansfield Motors	NE Militaria & Surplus	Pub Para-phernalia	Strange Fruits	Graphics Co.	Trophy Miniatures
Appeals to demographically narrow audience	0	1	1	½	1	½	½	½	½	½
Provides a genuinely useful product or service	0	1	1	1	1	½	1	0	1	1
Establishes a buyer-seller relationship & cust. loyalty	1	1	½	1	1	0	1	0	1	1
Uses technology judiciously	0	1	1	1	1	½	1	1	1	1
Focuses on customer's convenience — is user friendly	1	1	1	1	1	½	1	1	½	1
Provides an exclusive, bespoke or specialised prod. or service	1	1	½	1	1	1	1	1	1	1
Saves the customer money	0	1	1	½	1	½	1	0	0	1
Provides products or services difficult to acquire elsewhere	1	½	½	1	1	1	½	0	0	½
Adds value; provides info about products or services; is entertaining or makes purchasing more pleasurable	1	1	0	1	1	½	1	0	½	1
Has structures in place (such as a delivery system) to cope with any potential demand	0	1	1	1	1	½	1	0	0	1
Score (out of 10)	5*	9½	7½	9	10	5½	9	3½*	5½	9

* The case studies that gained a Strategic Fit score of 5 or less have all subsequently dropped their Net presence or are in the process of re-evaluating their Internet marketing business plan.

After just a year on this BT-sponsored e-commerce trial, Trophy Miniatures has broken all sales records in its 25-year history. Since joining the trial, orders for the company's figurines have increased by 62 per cent, requiring the company to employ more staff. The company has enjoyed a record year with orders from all over the world, 75 per cent of which are from the US. This significant change in profitability is directly due to its web presence.

Trophy Miniatures has turned a niche "hobby business" into a global player, with 2,500 product lines that are in demand in markets all over the world. However, the fourteen other small businesses that took part in the e-commerce trial, who do not offer goods or services that appeal to the Internet audience, saw no increase in sales.

This company is an emphatic example of how imperative it is that any firm considering going online should be a business with the correct strategic fit for Internet commerce. If it has, profits can be exceptional.

Part 2

Going Online

7

INTERNET EQUIPMENT AND CONNECTION

To get connected to the Internet two elements are required: equipment and an access account (see Chapter 8, Access to the Internet).

There are three pieces of equipment required:

- A computer (including peripherals)

- A modem (to connect your computer to a telephone line)

- An Internet connection (e.g. a telephone socket).

COMPUTERS

Using the Internet does not require a particularly powerful computer as you are only accessing images and text sent from a distant computer. The Internet can be accessed from any type of computer: a desktop, laptop or even a hand-held PDA (personal digital assistant). However, to get the fullest use of all the utilities available on the Internet the computer and modem you use should be the fastest you can afford. The faster your computer, modem, and Internet connection, the lower your overall costs for using the Internet will be. Naturally, your budget will play an important part in your decision-making, but the fastest machine you can afford may save you considerable cost in the long term.

When it comes to buying a computer for your business, the options range from either direct purchasing from major manufacturers, High Street retailers and mail order companies, or having a bespoke system assembled specifically for you with all necessary software pre-loaded. However, there are advantages in purchasing from a well-known brand or a local supplier. Big brand manufacturers tend to be more expensive but provide support and warrantees etc., while local suppliers tend to give better value for money and a faster response to any problems.

Buying a brand new machine just for the Internet may not be justified, therefore you may have to make sure that any machine you intend to use for Internet access is upgraded to the highest possible specifications affordable. Prices of computer components are falling constantly. The components that should be upgraded are:

- The Random Access Memory (RAM)

- The hard drive

- The processor

- The monitor.

The RAM is measured in megabytes (Mb). The more RAM your computer has the faster it will work. Most current computer software requires at least 32 Mb of RAM to run efficiently.

The hard drive is used to store your data. Storage is measured in megabytes (Mb) and gigabytes (Gb); a gigabyte is equivalent to 1,000 megabytes. Most computers now come with at least a 1GB hard drive.

The processor (central processing unit or CPU) drives the computer and its speed is measured in mega hertz (MHz). As stated previously, you do not need a particularly powerful machine to use the Internet, therefore, a processor of 233 MHz should be fast enough to cope with both current and future software and Internet use.

The monitor should preferably be a colour monitor, and have a S-VGA graphics adapter (which can display a resolution of at least 800 x 600 pixels). The higher the screen resolution, and the larger the monitor's screen, the greater the viewing area will be.

If you have a PC you should use Microsoft Windows as the operating system (O/S), and upgrade to either version '95 or '98, since most Internet software is now designed to run under Windows. Any new Macintosh can be connected to the Internet and you can connect older Macintoshes but you may need Apple's TCP/IP software. For either operating system, you may also need to acquire electronic mail software, WWW browser, newsgroup reader and FTP software, which should be available from your Internet Service Provider (ISP).

Although it may be comparatively simple to set up a business online, it may be a great deal more difficult to do it efficiently and cost effectively. Going online may be made more costly for a business venture when not all costs are apparent. The costs may seem comparatively modest, but the cost of start-up may represent a significant percentage of a small company's total capital, therefore try to budget accurately before over-spending on equipment you may not need.

If the business does not already own or have access to an up-to-date PC or Mac, a machine with the minimum specifications required for basic business and Internet use (32 RAM, 1Gb hard drive, 233MHz processor, 1Mb graphics card and 15in monitor),[1] the business will have to make a minimum investment of around £400 (€620) to £500 (€775).

MODEMS

The only other hardware required will be an internal or external modem and a phone line. The modem connects your computer, via a modem cable, to your phone socket. A modem converts data from a computer into sound signals that can then be transmitted over a normal telephone line; it works the opposite way around when receiving information. If you want to look at web pages that contain many graphic images you will need the fastest modem you can afford to download the data that makes up the images stored on your computer as a graphic image. Most current modems also support the fax standards. Ideally, your modem should be at least 56Kbps.

INTERNET CONNECTION

Internet connection packages vary considerably from one Internet access provider to another, and the range of services and prices change frequently, so any published information about the cost of linking to the Internet should be verified with a representative group of a number of telecommunications companies (telcos). As would be expected, the capacity and speed of the basic connection service will determine the cost of Internet access. The general rule is that the higher the bandwidth capacity and the faster the speed, the higher the cost to install and maintain the Internet link. Consequently, connections devoted to the use of one company are significantly more expensive than shared connections.

Companies can choose their Internet connection from three basic options. The least expensive connection is a *dial-up connection* to a local ISP shared line service, which may be billed on the basis of how many hours the connection is used each month. The connection is made directly through any existing phone socket. This connection would be recommended for most small owner-manager organisations (see Standard Telephone Lines below).

In the medium cost range is a *dedicated dial-up connection*, which can be run from a workstation with the appropriate software and at modem speeds over a regular telephone line, an ISDN line, or a leased line from a local ISP (see ISDN below).

The most expensive is a *dedicated connection*, which has the capacity to link an organisation directly to the Internet and will require the installation of network hardware on-site as well as a special leased line from an Internet system access provider (ISAP) (see Leased Lines below).

CHOOSING A TELEPHONE SERVICE

As stated in the previous section, there are three main kinds of Internet telephone line services:

- Standard telephone lines

- ISDN

- Leased lines.

Currently, of all commercial Internet connections in the EU, 41 per cent are via leased lines, 26 per cent via ISDN and 33 per cent are over standard telephone lines.

Standard Telephone Lines

For the vast majority of businesses a standard telephone line is all you need. It is the cheapest option and has a proven record of reliability. Unless you use a mobile phone for business calls you may require a second line, in addition to your main business telephone line, to avoid missing important business calls while using the modem. For the best usage, one line should be dedicated to Internet use. For an Internet-dedicated line, all you require is an ordinary telephone line linked to your computer which, ideally, would be dedicated to all your Internet activities. You will then easily be able to monitor usage of the Internet and calculate your usage costs.

Dial-up connections to an ISP are the least expensive option of all. Whenever you want to connect to the Internet, you dial the telephone number of the ISP. Every minute used during the Internet connection is billed to the telephone line. This type of connection combines ease of installation with the lowest prices available but without the advantages of a direct Internet connection. The one major drawback to lower speed connections is the limitations they place on access to the World Wide Web.

If limiting up-front costs is a priority then the connection itself can be scaled down to the speed and capacity needed in the short term, with an option to upgrade as Internet use increases. High-speed modem connections to the Internet, known as SLIP (Serial Line IP) and PPP (Point to Point Protocol) are also possible through a standard telephone line at much lower cost than ISDN or dedicated, leased lines. This type of connection requires instal-lation of the appropriate modem and software, and has limita-tions in terms of the number of users supported, and the speed of the connection, but many small companies have found it to be a cost-effective way to connect to the Internet.

Advantages:

- Inexpensive
- Ease of installation
- Reliability.

Disadvantages:

- Lower speed connections
- Lower logon dependability
- Possible connection interference.

ISDN

ISDN (Integrated Services Digital Network) is a completely digital telephone line supplied by telcos and has been the standard tele-phone line in countries such as Germany for some time. Being a digital line, it does not require a modem.

There are now a number of hybrid analogue and ISDN serv-ices, which give users two ISDN channels without having to up-grade their analogue lines or change their existing telephone number. Aimed at small businesses and tele-workers, these lines use on-site hardware to enable the user's existing phone lines to access digital and analogue services at the same time. The technology involves splitting an existing phone line into two channels, analogue or digital. As with ISDN, two digital channels can be bonded together to form a single virtual 128Kbps channel, although this does incur a double time charge.

Many telcos now provide all the services a business needs from the Internet within the environment of a "virtual trade park". For example, they may provide a web site (including design packages) with integrated communications for e-mail, fax and voice messages, as well as online information services that are relevant to business, including news and trade events and company credit checking.

Companies such as Deutsche Telecom are also providing broader bandwidth lines, such as ADSL (Asymmetric Digital Subscriber Line), which offer a data rate of 8Mbps. As Internet access increases in the future, and the demand for broadband technologies increases, we are likely to see a demand for cheaper broad bandwidth technologies.

Advantages:

- Each ISDN line is effectively a double line allowing you to use the Internet and make a phone call at the same time.

- ISDN connections are very fast, reducing connection periods and call charges.

- ISDN connections reduce interference.

Disadvantages:

- ISDN line installation charges are more expensive.

- ISDN line rental fees are more expensive.

- ISDN line access charges are more expensive.

- ISDN line users need to be close to an ISDN exchange.

- ISDN line users may need to upgrade their computer.

Before you install ISDN, make sure that your ISP supports an ISDN link, as many online service providers (OSPs) do not. However, the majority of the bigger ISPs will let you link via ISDN for an extra installation fee.

Leased Lines

The next step up from an ISDN connection is to install a leased line between you and the ISP. When using a leased line, you do not use a modem or an ISDN adapter; instead you need to install a router. A router is the software that routes access to the Internet to and from a network of computers (see Chapter 8, Access to the Internet: Network Installation). This software ensures that the data from your computer is correctly formatted and addressed before it is sent to the Internet. A separate router computer costs around £1,000 (€1,550), though operating systems such as Windows 98 have router capacity for up to five workstations. Again, you need to check that your ISP supports this service as few presently do.

For the basic service of a leased line, there is little speed advantage over an ISDN link as both run at a speed of at least 64,000 bits per second. A leased line is a standard telephone line that is permanently "open". A line has no number and no one can make another call. The leased line allows your computer to be permanently connected to the Internet.

Companies that will frequently send large amounts of data through the Internet, or that need to connect a number of workstations and users, should consider their own dedicated line, which is leased through a network provider. There will be start-up costs for the line installation and purchase of networking equipment; these costs and the annual fee will vary with the size and complexity of the site and the speed of connection.

There are no telephone charges with a leased line. Instead, you pay a quarterly rental, if you are close to a major city, or more if you are at a greater distance. Leased lines are expensive and are only cost effective for firms that conduct a considerable amount of Internet-related work, want to connect their own Internet server to the Internet and so need to provide a 24-hour link, or are a large company with considerable financial resources. If your company has a large number of users or you want to connect your office network to the Internet, you might find it cheaper to install a leased line than to pay a telephone bill.

Advantages:

- Connections are very fast, reducing connection times.

- Low connection interference.

Disadvantages:

- There is little speed advantage over an ISDN link.

- Installation charges are expensive.

- Rental fees are expensive.

- Line users need to be close to an exchange (Internet access point or hub).

- Line users may need to upgrade their computers.

REFERENCES

---

[1] *PC Direct* magazine, March 1998, p. 135.

8

ACCESS TO THE INTERNET

Once you have an appropriate computer and modem set up, you will need to choose an access account so that you can access the Internet. Most small businesses only require a dial up account over a standard telephone line, so the company will not be permanently connected to the Internet. You then simply "dial up" to the Internet, through your ISP, when you need to.

Companies that provide you with an access account to use the Internet are known as "access providers", "service providers" or Internet service providers (ISPs). No ISP is of use to a specific business if it does not provide the services that that business requires. Most small owner-manager businesses will benefit from a cheap-rate local dial-up connection number. Therefore, before any contract is signed with an ISP, a check should be made with the firm's telephone company to confirm that a single nation-wide access number is to be used, charged at local rate, as otherwise Internet connections could be charged at expensive long-distance call rates.

As one of your biggest on-going expenses for using the Internet will be telephone costs you should use an Internet access account that enables cheaper local phone calls to your ISP to be made. It should also be taken into account that all telecos charge for each dial-up connection to the Internet.

For a local call facility you will require an ISP that has a local "point of presence" (POP). *Yellow Pages* now has an "Internet Services" category, which should include local access providers.

Internet magazines also contain listings of access providers and indicate whether or not there is a POP near you. Most computer dealers should be able to inform you as to where any local ISPs are. Most ISPs have POPs in major metropolitan areas.

The service from an ISP is similar to a phone rental; the payment is of a fixed amount to the ISP every month. In return, a firm can dial into the ISP's network via a modem and connect the firm's computer to the Net. Most European ISPs still charge a start-up fee to create an Internet account, typically between £10 (€15) and £20 (€30), and most rely on regular payments of between £5 (€8) and £20 (€30) a month to maintain the service. This almost always includes some web space, so your firm can advertise on the Net.

A badly performing ISP can seriously affect your company's online performance. For example, domestic services can suffer from incoming and outgoing e-mail delays, limited e-mail quotas (typically 1.5Mb, which is too little to allow for high-resolution images or photographs), and slow download speeds, especially when viewing US sites. All this adds up to a hidden cost for dial-up users. Time and money spent on research into the company's eventual choice of ISP may pay for itself in terms of a reliable and robust connection (see Choosing an ISP below).

Most ISPs can supply an all-in-one package that includes all the software needed, typically a web browser and perhaps cut-down news and e-mail clients too. If these are unsuitable, alternatives are widely available on the Web and are free to download. However, monthly running costs can be comparatively high, depending on usage, such as regular web browsing during office hours, as well as e-mail. Businesses that mainly use e-mail and only occasionally venture on to the Web will pay much less.

The variable costs of using the Internet will include the amount of time a company is online. Unlike in the US, where local rate telephone calls are free, very few phone companies in the EU offer free calls to ISPs. According to market research firm Ovum, this situation is very unlikely to change within the next two years.[1] However, following the lead of the US, the UK is now starting to witness a limited number of small telcos offering free local calls on weekends and weekdays after 6.00 pm.

Along with small independent telcos, now larger companies, such as British Telecom, are planning to introduce a "free phone" service to their own Internet service. It is hoped that the rest of the EU telcos will follow this initiative but until ISPs develop new and alternative methods of revenue generation, such as targeted advertising or charging a commission on web-generated sales, European companies will have to pay for Internet access.

If immediate access is essential to your particular business then you should consider signing up to two ISPs. In the not uncommon event that your preferred ISP's server becomes inaccessible, you can log on to your reserve ISP. Another ISP may also offer other advantages such as free services, larger web space or more e-mail addresses, which may be of use to your particular type of business. Another advantage would be in the event of a security breach on one of your servers.

CHOOSING AN ISP

For small businesses and sole traders there are more than 100 ISPs to choose between, from small local providers to large global service providers. There are two main tiers of ISPs. The largest are the international and national ISPs. These have large networks with large bandwidths, many POPs, and access to a greater part of the Internet as a whole. There are also the smaller regional and local providers that typically buy *backbone* access from the larger ISPs. Each depends on the larger provider for access to the Internet as a whole.

Large national ISPs, or online services, lease lines that connect directly to the main backbone of the Internet (see Using Online Service Providers). Regional providers in turn lease lines from the nationals. Individuals cannot access the backbone directly, only through an ISP. If an ISP is peered with a number of large networks and they, in turn, are peered with more large networks, data has a greater chance of being shuttled to its destination at speed.

Most ISPs allow a trial period of (usually) a month before insisting on a long-term contract of (usually) a year. This allows customers an opportunity to use the numerous free trial offers available before deciding on an ISP.

Most ISPs also provide users with a customised version of Microsoft's Internet Explorer.5, which is best on Windows 95 and 98, and nearly all provide Netscape Communicator.4. Businesses going online should enquire as to which software is required (as working around browser incompatibilities can add 25 per cent to the cost of a web site),[2] how is it installed, whether it is provided by the ISP and if any extra payment is required. Enquiries should also be made as to whether support is available and if it is available outside normal office hours. Technical support lines may be free, local call rate, or national call rate, all of which may add to overall costs.

The level of services provided should suit your specific business needs. If the business only wants e-mail facilities, or access to the World Wide Web, it should not have to subscribe to other facilities such as a consulting service. Other facilities provided may include free space for a company web site, though there may be a charge per megabyte beyond the default allotment (usually 5 to 25Mbs). There may also be a restriction on the amount of hits a company is allowed each month.

Some service providers have a low monthly charge but only give a limited number of online hours per month. Enquiries should be made as to the ISP's billing policy. It may bill by the second, have a minimum charge per call or round-up the logged time for each connection. If the company builds a web site, note should be taken as to whether extra charges are based on the amount of traffic that site generates.

In the final analysis, the main measure of an ISP's technical worth is speed. Transfer rates vary from the slower 14.4 and 56Kbps modems to the faster velocity DS3/T3 (64Mbps) leased lines. If an ISP has too few modems and there is difficulty connecting, this is a "speed hit". If an ISP cannot handle the data load there will be a speed hit. If the ISP is connected to low bandwidth lines there will be also be a speed hit. From the user's point of view an ISP's performance is judged by the amount of time taken to open a web site, download a file or connect to a site. Therefore ISPs should be committed to providing a minimum of 56Kbps speed lines.

The most common reason for slow connections on the Net is not congestion but dropped data packets. Data is split into small pieces and encapsulated in "packets" before it leaves a computer. Each packet contains important information necessary to move data and identify its content. The packet has a limited life expectancy based on the number of routers it goes through. The most important job for Internet routers is to sort each packet and send it on until it gets to its destination.

Depending on an ISP's network peering, the packet may have to go through many of these routers before its destination. If too many routers (also known as hops) are encountered a data packet may become extinct, requiring it to be re-sent. The result is frequently slow or dropped connections. For reference, users may request a list of an ISP's peers and network topology map of its network.

Modem to User Ratio

This is a reflection of the size of the company. The more customers an ISP has, the more lines and modems it needs. If an ISP has a low ratio of modems to users, there may well be a delay to get connected to the Internet. For serious business use you need an

ISP that provides instant access, which requires a high ratio of modems to users. Most access providers publish their ratios, as it is a means of identifying the best company to opt for.

ISP Registration Fees

Increasingly, there is a move towards free access to the Internet, with more and more companies offering free services, though, as noted earlier, very few telcos presently offer free line use. Some companies still ask you to pay a fee to register with them. This fee covers the initial administration of setting up your account etc. Some companies charge a large initial fee and then low ongoing fees. Others charge larger ongoing fees, but no set up charges. Some companies charge a one-off cost "for life". You have to make the choice according to your company's Internet budget and long-term economic position. However, if you are going to be using the Internet more than a couple of times a week, perhaps you should choose the firms that have higher initial charges and lower ongoing costs, as this will make your per minute usage costs lower (see Appendix 3).

Ongoing Costs

Some companies will charge you fees on a monthly basis; others on an annual basis. Some charge you per minute, based on the length of your connection time. Generally, you get lower fees if you pay annually in advance. Those that charge you per minute can work out very expensive. There is a tendency for companies to underestimate the amount of time they will be connected to the Internet. Therefore, if you budget for a particular amount of Internet-related charges based on the "per minute" charge, you could end up paying considerably more, often more than would have been the case with monthly or annual billing.

According to a recent report published by Datamonitor,[3] of all European countries UK Internet users currently pay the highest monthly access charges in Europe. According to the report, entitled *PC-based Internet access markets in Europe, 1998-2003: Surviving Market Consolidation,* UK Internet users pay on average £15.42 (€24) per month to service providers (see Appendix 6).

Software Provision

The set-up fees that you pay an ISP should include the costs of the relevant computer software that you need to surf the Web (such as Netscape's *Navigator*.4 or Microsoft's *Internet Explorer*.5). These programs work on all the mainstream business computers. Your ISP should provide and configure all Internet-connection software for you. The software required to set-up a commercial site, including payment facilities, costs around £100 (€155).

User Support

The issue of service back-up, should anything go wrong, is something that is rarely thought of until it is too late. An ISP should constantly monitor its network's performance and have contingency plans in place for network outages. It should have built-in redundancy (spare capacity in the event of an emergency), and on-site back-ups for its servers. Back-up generators should also be in place in case of power failure, and generators should keep any necessary equipment functioning for a reasonable time. An ISP should be able to cope with any service failure and preferably have a back up Network Operations Centre (NOC).

In order to remain competitive, many ISPs have started to offer more substantial educational and training programs, customised security arrangements, and other services tailored for business customers, as part of their user support facilities. Training can be especially important for organisations without the facilities, resources and cash for in-house training programs as training and maintenance can represent the highest costs of an Internet presence (see section on Training later in this chapter). It is in the interest of every business to talk to several potential providers before making a decision about an Internet connection.

You should ask potential ISPs what kinds of user support they provide. For example, in addition to training, having online user-help can be very useful. You may have to pay higher ongoing fees for higher levels of support, so you need to balance your finances with your requirements.

USING ONLINE SERVICE PROVIDERS

There are a number of online service providers (OSPs) that provide access to the Internet, often through a local POP. They are known as OSPs to distinguish them from the smaller ISPs. These online companies are commercial concerns that have their own databases and information services for their own subscribers to access in addition to getting onto the Internet. There are three[*] global online services providing Internet access:

- AOL (America On-Line)
- CompuServe
- MSN (Microsoft Network).

There are also country-specific online services, such as the UK's Virgin Net. All of these online services provide a host of features of their own, in addition to Internet access. They have electronic mail, databases on all sorts of topics, and special interest groups for discussions and information exchange. However, even added together, these online services do not provide anywhere near the amount of material that is available on the whole Internet, which is why they have to provide access to the Internet in addition to their own services.

If an OSP provides you with a specific business facility that is not available elsewhere, then it will obviously be of advantage to you to use it. However, if you are only using the service as a means of getting onto the Internet, OSPs tend to work out more

[*] AOL and CompuServe are now both part of the same company.

expensive for Internet access than using a direct link through an ISP. This may not always be true; it depends upon the amount of time you will be using the Internet compared with the online company's own services which, initially, will be difficult to evaluate.

As mentioned previously, the most popular and cost effective method used to evaluate an Internet service is to use the numerous free trial memberships available. These provide time-limited access to the online services and the Internet. Every month at least one ISP offers a free trial of this kind. These trials provide a useful way of finding out what each online service has to offer as well as what is advantageous to your particular business on the Internet (see Appendix 3).

THE MODEL ISP

The model ISP would provide a one-month, no obligation free trial, and with no set up charges. Costs should be free or no greater than £12 (€18) per month (including VAT). Ideally an ISP should offer 15Mbs to 25Mbs of free web space and five e-mail addresses. Support should include local-call access, telephone technical support after 6.00 pm and at weekends. Many ISPs deliver CD-ROMs with software (including Navigator.4 or Internet Explorer.5) that has a simple automatic installation procedure. Though this model represents the ideal ISP, in reality ISPs are, at present, usually less generous (see Appendix 3).

In the UK, *Freeserve* is an Internet service from Dixons (including PC World outlets). It was the first European ISP to eliminate monthly subscription fees, and is now the UK's biggest provider of access to the Net with over 1.5 million users. There are now an increasing amount of ISPs offering free Internet access, e.g. X-Stream, BT Click+, Indigo (Ireland) and FreeUK. FreeUK (www.freeuk.co.uk) is one of the latest UK ISPs and offers unlimited access, 25Mb of web space and 24-hour technical support.

The only differences between these free-access providers and fee-charging ISPs are domain name or e-mail address limitations and cost. Most free-access providers insist on you using their name in your domain name and e-mail addresses, which can look less professional to potential customers. However, free-access providers cost nothing except the phone call.

CHECKLIST FOR CHOOSING A SERVICE PROVIDER

Selecting an Internet service provider and determining the most appropriate Internet connection to support your particular business objectives should involve a consideration of all the options available. It may help if you e-mail each ISP with a checklist of questions to be answered before you decide on which would be the most beneficial and appropriate to your specific business needs. Questions might look for information on the following areas:

- Its location.

- Its modem to user ratio.

- Its registration fees.

- Its ongoing fees.

- Its modem transfer rate (e.g. 56Kbps).

- Its reliability record.

- Does it have back-up generators?

- How does it maintain its network?

- Which Browser software does it use (i.e. IE.5 or Netscape.4)?

- Does it provide all necessary software?

- Does it provide online user help and is it provided outside office hours?

- Its charge rates for user support.

- Does it charge for web space above the normal allotment?

- Does it limit the number of hits each month?

- Does it limit the number of online hours per month?

- Does it bill by the second, minute or hour?

- Does it have a minimum charge per call?

- Its customisation options.

- Its ease of installation and use of software.

- Its total customer base and percentage of business customers.

- Its size range and number of small business customers.

- Its number of commercial customers using each type of connection (dedicated, dial-up, shared access, etc.).

- Its total annual costs in each category of connection and service for small businesses.

- Your responsibilities as a customer for equipment operation and maintenance.

- The level of training available and its costs.

- The accessibility of other networks through the connection.

- The security options and their cost.

GOING ONLINE

Once you have decided on your host ISP, domain names and e-mail addresses, and the way your Internet activities will be managed, you are ready to set-up your ISP's software. Apple Macintosh computers have a different operating system from PCs and need different Internet access software. New Apple Macs, including the latest, the iMac, have connections to specific Internet services pre-installed.

A good ISP will normally send you an Internet set-up CD disc, or floppy disc if necessary, with easy-to-follow instructions, backed up by a support line if you have any questions. You should be able to simply insert the disc into a computer and then follow a series of straightforward on-screen instructions that will guide you through the set-up process. Within a few minutes you should be successfully online.

The software should be set-up according to your company's needs, including its e-mail addresses. You should also alter any pre-set preferences so that they match your requirements. For instance, some programs may pre-set the interval for checking for electronic mail to every ten or twenty minutes. If you only receive a few e-mails per week, this can be expensive. Changing to a longer interval (perhaps every 720 minutes) would allow your computer to only automatically dial once a day, unless you had already done so.

Once all software and facilities are set as you require, and your modem is switched on, it can be cost effective to leave these on permanently as they do not use up much electricity. With the modem on you can dial up to the Internet, follow the software installation instructions, and initiate any Internet commerce.

THE COST OF GOING ONLINE

The approximate minimum costs for a small business with 1 to 2 users would be as follows:

Hardware — Modem	£80.00
— Dedicated phone line	£99.00
Software — (provided by ISP)	Free
— Commercial software	£100.00
Extras — ISP set-up cost	Free
— Annual maintenance	£100.00
Registration fees and domain name	£75.00

Training (for one person)	£250.00
Instructional books, magazines, etc.	£75.00
Total set-up costs (including £500.00 computer)	£1,269.00*
Total monthly costs	£110.00

* Average price as of June 1999 (does not include anti-virus software which is highly recommended).

NETWORK INSTALLATION

Networks (intranets or internal Internets) are only necessary for small organisations with a number of computers. A network is a means of connecting together workstations, file servers, and printers within an organisation in order that software, printers, and authorised data may be shared. However, any new network installation should be driven by strategic business requirements rather than on a technological basis. Technology should not be used for its own sake.

The process of choosing all the right components for a network is vital in order to deliver the services that the business needs, including future needs. The network has to be able to develop, to grow not only in size and capacity but also in speed and performance. Servers and operating systems need to be chosen specifically to match the applications and usage to which they are going to be put. The overriding factor is that the whole service delivery has to be seamless, robust, expandable and, most importantly, secure and supportable.

The amount of work that setting up and managing a network requires should not be underestimated. Even using sophisticated infrastructure tools to assist the ongoing support function requires high levels of knowledge, expertise and time during the initial setting-up phases and throughout the lifetime of the system. Many organisations look to outsource the maintenance and management of networks to address these problems, and are buying in a service, as they do with electricity and telephony.

If your company decides to install a network it is essential to consider whether to free up in-house IT specialists. These staff, who have the necessary knowledge and experience of the business, may have to work on added-value projects that improve competitive advantage, rather than on generic IT functions such as support or network management. Management should view the network as a means of increasing business efficiency by speeding up time-consuming internal processes, decreasing time-to-market, and improving competitive advantage.

For larger companies requiring e-commerce capability, the usual option for connecting to the world is the traditional leased line, available in capacities which range from 64Kbps through to 2Mbps and beyond (see Chapter 7, Internet Equipment and Connection: Choosing a Telephone Service). A flat fee for access or a payment per megabyte of traffic per line can be made. If Frame Relay or SMDS capability already exists on your corporate network, a telco will be able to hook an Internet link into these existing facilities.

When choosing the link to the Internet, thought should be made not only about today's requirements but also about future needs. Adding more bandwidth to a leased line does not mean adding more physical connections. For example, moving from 64 Kbps to 256Kbps requires adding software controls, not installing a bigger pipe. As a rough guide, a 64Kbps link costs around £10,000 (€15,5000) a year, after a £1,000 (€1,550) to £2,000 (€3,000) set-up charge, including a managed router at your end. At the other end of the scale, the cost may be a £3,000 (€4,500) to £4,000 (€6,000) set-up fee plus £40,000 (€60,000) for the annual rental of a 2Mbps link. These costs make permanent Net access prohibitive to most small firms.

INTERNET SERVERS

A *server* is a system of computers or software dedicated to providing a facility or service on a network. Once any connection decisions have been finalised, the decision has to be made as to what computers and web server software is to be used. The two main options are Unix and Windows NT. NT is becoming very popular in the IT world at the moment; it is robust and it will look familiar to anyone who has ever used Windows applications. Windows 98 also has limited networking capabilities.

Unix is the other popular web server platform. It is less user-friendly than NT, and is only recommended for those who have the experience or the time and inclination to learn it properly. There are several different versions of Unix; the popular ones for web serving are Solaris, Sun's version of Unix, and Linux (a free version of Unix for PCs), which most experts agree works very efficiently.

As regards the hardware, Macintoshes and Linux-based PCs are very popular as low-end servers. NT is more resource-hungry and so will not run on older computers such as 386s. Nevertheless, if the company were to be upgrading a fairly sizeable machine elsewhere on the network, something that used to be, for example, a NetWare fileserver, it would make a good NT-based web server.

IT is a traditional problem area for emerging small businesses that need the use of a network, but do not need the expense or complication commonly involved. The obvious way to overcome this is to invest in one of the many network starter kits on the market, all of which promise to provide a cheap and easy-to-use network. The general small business owner-manager, however, is unlikely to have the time, or inclination, to configure all the network kit without professional instruction.

SERVER SOFTWARE

As far as the server software is concerned, under NT Microsoft's *Internet Information Server* (IIS), and Windows 98, it can be run for free. Under Unix, there are various free, information-holding servers, the most popular of which is Apache. There are also commercial applications. Netscape produces a variety of server software, for both NT and Unix (the NT version is less expensive). Apache has a commercial incarnation, called *StrongHold*. There is also *Purveyor* (NT) and a fleet of less commonly used software, including Novell's offering for NetWare servers. Thought should also be given to the compatibility of any other software intended for use on the system. For example, if a back-end database is planned, it will affect (and be affected by) the choice of hardware and server software.

TRAINING

If your Internet-based venture is going to succeed, you may have staff that will need to be trained. This may sound obvious but a recent report revealed that a quarter of European e-commerce ventures fail due to lack of understanding and support. The survey, *Business on the Web* by Cambridge Intelligence Unit (CIU), showed that among Europe's largest corporations, almost a quarter of e-commerce projects are abandoned before completion. For most, failure was not simply a result of a lack of investment. Around 18 per cent of companies with unsuccessful systems had set aside more than £2 million for the projects!

As important as the money spent on the software, the equipment, the network links, and the staff necessary to get a web site up and running, is the need for information on the site being kept up-to-date. If the company is presenting its product range or price list on the Web, it is essential that the site be updated regularly with current and accurate prices and products. Any staff and equipment should be budgeted to carry out the updates and maintenance of the site. The right staff, the right suppliers and the right set of hardware and software, which has a sensible upgrade path, are the prerequisites of a cost effective and competitive web site presence. All these elements could be co-ordinated to within a specific strategic plan and development time span, of perhaps two to five years. For a single owner-manager these elements are much more difficult to co-ordinate and maintain.

INTERNET PLANNING

Once you have chosen the kind of telephone service you require, and selected your ISP, you will need a written plan to guide you through your Internet usage. Simply establishing an Internet presence may not be enough; to do so can be costly, as it could waste staff time and increase all sorts of expenses for your business. So, the first step in going online is writing your Internet business plan. Without some kind of plan for using the Internet your business could suffer "strategic drift" and lower profit margins through increased telephone call costs etc.

Any Internet plan should be integrated into your company's overall business plan. A first step may be to make a staff member within the business responsible for all Internet-related activities. The Internet has the potential to be a highly valuable business tool in your firm, so it should be managed properly. Someone who is in charge of your company's Internet activities will therefore be able to ensure that you meet the requirements of your overall business strategy.

A key decision for the manager of an Internet-based business is how the company will be addressed in electronic mail messages. If everyone in the company has a different style, the outside world might not realise that you are all working together. Consistency is important and you need to decide how you will be addressed right at the start. A policy should be developed, whether you decide all your staff should have their mail addressed to their first name only, without surnames, or with their surnames and departments listed. Consistency will help deliver e-mail to the correct people and will also mean that your company, and its staff, is much more easily identifiable. It will also provide a professional corporate image to potential customers.

References

[1] *ComputerActive*, 13 August, 1998, p. 19

[2] *Computing*, 22 April, 1999, p. 20

[3] *PC Weekly*, 26 January, 1999, p. 4.

9

PLANNING AN INTERNET PRESENCE

DOMAIN NAMES

Once your web site is ready and available at your ISP it can be accessed by anyone in the world. However, to do this the page will need a domain name. These web addresses (or URLs) are agreed internationally, on a first-come, first-served basis, through America's InterNIC before permission of use is given to any company. InterNIC currently registers over 10,000 domain names per day, charging a £43 (€66) fee on each registration. Each registration currently takes three to seven days to confirm and lasts for two years.

An appropriate online name and address are essential to any Internet-based business if it is to be found easily by potential customers. Online, your brand is your URL. Therefore, even if your company is not yet ready for an Internet presence, you should register all relevant names now to stop other companies using it. To register any name(s) now will prove less expensive than buying it back from "cyber-squatters", or "speculators" who buy up company names hoping to sell them back to companies with an ethical right to them.

Your company domain name should be a name or product brand name that your customers will recognise you by. If at all possible, it should be an easily remembered name, such as www.yourname.com, rather than www.yourisp.com/~your name.etc. If you can afford the extra expense, it may be worth registering similar domain names to your own, including more than one suffix (e.g. .com and .co.ie), in case potential customers are not sure of your address or type it incorrectly.

Also, if your company is new or will be based exclusively on the Internet, it is worth considering a domain name that may have sexual connotations (see Chapter 10, Attracting and Keeping Customers: Sex Sells). If it has not already been taken, you should also try to register your name(s) with the more prestigious .com suffix.

PLATE 9.1: UK INTERNIC

As the restrictions on domain name eligibility are lifted, more and more previously unavailable domain name suffixes will become available. Country-specific suffixes may be used in creating online brand names that fit the industry your business operates in. Suffixes such as .tv (Tulvula) and .fm (Micronesia), may well be worth multimedia companies acquiring, whereas suffixes such as .md (Moldova), .co (Colombia) and .tm (Turkmenistan) all have obvious uses for companies in the appropriate market sectors.

If your company is more well known for the name of a product or service you provide, then you should consider registering it

separately, as well as your company's name, e.g. www.viagra.com
(the product) as well as www.pfizer.com (the company). It is predicted that of the 100 million registered domain names expected
world-wide by the year 2003, 27 million will be for products and
services.

Your address will usually contain the country, such as .uk or
.ie, from which your company originates. The exception is the
.com address, which has no international identification on the
Internet. The .com address most often means the organisation is in
the US, but in fact there is no way of knowing which makes it a
truly "universal" address. This is one reason why .com suffixes
are the most prestigious. Web addresses with the suffix of any
country you want can be bought, but taxes etc may be charged in
the country your company resides in (see Chapter 12, Electronic
Payments: Taxation).

The second part of the address, from the right, will identify
your particular type of organisation. These suffixes include the
following:

- .co = company (followed by a country e.g. .co.ie = an Irish
  company)

- .com = commercial organisation (mainly US)

- .org = non-commercial organisation

- .edu = educational establishment (mainly US)

- .ac = academic establishment

- .mu = military establishment

- .gov = government or government department

- .net= networks and ISPs (now used by many other Internet-
  based companies).

Most business addresses include the .co abbreviation, indicating
they are a commercial concern. The first part of the address for

web pages is usually www. Between www. and the .co is where your company's name, brand name or product will appear. You will be required by the international naming committee to come up with a word that reflects your business. To obtain your chosen URL you need to apply for it. There are two ways of doing this. You can get your ISP to make an application on your behalf, or you can apply yourself. To make your own application you need to contact one of the naming agencies which can be found on the Internet. One of the most popular is www.netnames.co.uk. Your ISP can register your domain name and rent you the necessary web space to host it.

The laws of intellectual property determine that domain names that correspond to a famous brand cannot be used.[1] Internet domain name registration web sites will help determine which domain names are already in use.[2] If the domain name is not already in use, then any new company names will have to be registered with InterNIC, the international body that administers the domain name system.[3]

The Internet's address book system is the Internet Assigned Numbers Authority (IANA). The IANA system tells computers where to route Internet traffic by matching the unique addresses (URLs) of up to 12 digits assigned to each computer on the Net. For example, the digital address 195.67.49.25 leads to search engine Yahoo!'s site, though it is easier to remember it as www.yahoo.com. Nominet is the non-profit making registration authority for Internet domain names ending in .uk. Network Solutions (NSI) registers top-level domain names such as .com. However, all interests of the global Internet community will soon be managed by the Internet Corporation for Assigned Names and Numbers (ICANN).

Business ISPs offer full domain name administration and mapping (e.g. www.yourname.com instead of www.yourname. yourisp.com); 20Mb+ of managed web space (including fast servers, CGI and statistics, support and regular back-ups); and unlimited e-mail accounts. Prices are typically around £200 (€300) a year, although these vary by up to £100 (€150) either way and do not always include dial-up or ISDN access, which has been bought from traditional ISPs at the usual rates. Other business options include multimedia feeds, secure servers for credit card transactions, and other e-commerce facilities.

Domain names are usually priced for two years and can be registered in over 200 countries. The most prestigious suffixes tend to be the US domains (i.e. .com) and currently cost approximately £29 (€45) to £65 (€100). The cost of other countries' domain names varies a great deal, based largely on demand.

Some companies, such as Web Provider (www.webprovider. com), offer free domain name registration, free hosting and free web space. However, companies such as these may use your site for advertising or use their name in your URL, i.e. www.yourname.webprovider.com. Domain names such as these are less expensive but do not provide a small company with as desirable an online corporate image as a www.yourname.com.

For a small business wanting to look bigger online, and can afford the extra expenditure, business-orientated ISP packages provide a more professional net presence. They may also provide a more cost-effective solution than an in-house web server running on a leased line, but still represent a significant investment. Added to set up fees, business ISP charges may still represent a significant financial cost to a small business, therefore all costs should be calculated before any commitment.

WHAT IS A WEB SITE?

Before you plan an Internet presence you should be sure how you want your business to be represented on the Web and what you want your web site to look like and do for you. You should be sure what a web site actually is and what are the limits of its functionality.

A web site is a collection of separate pages (some companies have just a couple of pages, others have tens of thousands). These pages are stored as text files that contain special formatting codes that describe how the text looks when displayed. These codes, called HTML (hypertext mark-up language), describe the size, colour and font of text together with any images, sound or video clips. Lastly, and most important, the HTML codes describe hypertext links that allow a user to navigate from one page to another.

Each web page on a site may be made up of the following files:

• An HTML file that contains text, links to other pages and HTML formatting codes

• Graphic files that contain images, background patterns, icons or photographs all stored in GIF (graphic file format) or the JPEG file format

• Data files to provide a searchable data source

• Sound files to provide sound for your web pages

• Scripts that allow you to add functions to your web pages.

The only file you really need is a file that contains HTML codes. These are full of the text you want to display together with HTML commands that describe the way in which the text should be formatted on a static web page.

The individual pages of a web site are called web pages and are normally stored in separate document files. Each web page has a filename and is stored on your section of your ISP's hard disk. If you have decided to install your own Internet server in your company, then your web pages will be stored on your own server.

Any user with a web browser can now enter your URL (Uniform Resource Locator) that uniquely identifies where on the Internet your web pages are stored and view them. Any formatted text that you included in the web page will be sent to the user and displayed in exactly the same format you set up. If you included images in the web page, they will be transferred over the Internet to the user and displayed on the user's screen.

There is no *one* way to develop a web site; it is a case of identifying the type of web site that is best suited to your specific business. Small firms with regional services or niche products either need a cheap and quick solution or no web presence at all. If a web presence is to be invested in there are some issues that have to be addressed, most importantly cost effectiveness.

Making the decision to set up and maintain a web site is not easy; it takes a considerable amount of time, money and effort to design, create and maintain a good, informative web site. Before you start any of the design or construction of a site, you must first decide what you want your web site to achieve for the company.

The following are the three basic formats your web site can take:

1. A corporate catalogue

2. A marketing site

3. An interactive site.

The choice of web site format will determine the money, effort and marketing required to set up and maintain the site.

A Corporate Catalogue

This is the simplest, least functional web site format. It provides a potential customer with your company, product and service details — an electronic catalogue. It could also include lists of distributors or contacts where a customer might find your products. These sites are the simplest to set up and maintain but are also the least interesting for the visitor.

A Marketing Site

This second type of web site provides all the basic information about your company and its products and services, but also offers more to the potential customer. It could include a simple search function that allows visitors to look for particular information stored in archived material, or demonstration software or utilities available for download. It could also have a simple electronic questionnaire or formats to permit customers to ask for more information and provide vital customer feedback.

This type of site needs regular maintenance to keep the information up to date, and you will need to respond to any questionnaires or queries sent by electronic mail. The site will take more effort to design and set up, as it includes links to other pages and perhaps to other sites that could be useful to customers.

An Interactive Site

This web site format includes most web design features. It allows a visitor to browse your product range and also offers secure methods for payment of goods. It could have a link to a company database that allows users to query the database for information. It should also provide added-value elements such as information or entertainment, or at least be an attractive and efficient site to use.

Ideally, a fully interactive site such as this would be based on an in-house Internet server and would need to be monitored full-time to ensure that the database links are working, that any queries or electronic mail messages get a response and that customers purchasing goods actually receive them.

Once you have determined what you want your web site to achieve, you can set a budget for its development. You could put up a web site for just a few pounds per month using an ISP to do all the hard work. There are plenty of small businesses, which have set up simple sites that offer basic functions to customers. If you create and manage the site in your own time, you could create a professional looking and fully functional site for around £1,000 (€1,500) per year.

As a means of corporate branding, distribution, marketing and advertising, a web site can be relatively inexpensive and therefore cost-effective. The Internet is unparalleled in its ability to reach a target audience. It also has the flexibility to react to customer requirements automatically. However, existing and prospective customers will inevitably be reluctant to use a poorly designed, slow, or difficult to navigate site. This does not mean your web site needs to be hugely expensive, however, depending on what business functions it is designed to fulfil.

DESIGNING A WEB SITE

The following steps should be included when designing a web site:

1. Deciding what to include

2. Organising the content

3. Planning the layout

4. Choosing the hyperlinks

5. Checking that content is legal

6. Testing the web site's functionality.

Deciding What to Include

The first step requires selecting what company and product information should be included. If you have an established business, you have to look at the way your company already does business and replicate it on the Web. Work out who your customers are and the manner in which they like to do business with you; the web site should, as far as possible, feel familiar to existing customers when they use it for the first time.

Most companies use a combination of one or more of the following elements for their web site content: company mission statement, company history, company profile, products and services offered, staff profiles, customer lists, testimonials from customers, hot links to customers' web sites, hot links to suppliers' web sites, hot links to professional or trade associations, hot links to relevant subject areas, hot links to ISPs, hot links to the web site designer, etc.

Some of the following content suggestions may be of use but not all of them are essential:

- Relevant company information (as well as membership of trade organisations, etc.).

- All company products should be described or illustrated in full.

- All prices, including taxes, handling and shipping costs.

- Any special offers or positive price comparisons should be included.

- If appropriate, a value-added service or entertainment feature should be offered.

- Pictures, graphics, colours and sounds should fit the company image.

- An appropriate degree of customer interaction should be included.

- Methods should be used to gather customer data, comments, and information.

The size, functionality or information which can be included in a web site is limited by the size of computer memory available for storing it. A web site with photos, graphics, animation and sound requires a great deal of memory. Each section should therefore be brief and to the point so that it requires as few pages as possible. If your site is kept simple and elegantly designed it will download, read and print more easily. This will reduce customers' viewing costs and your company's ISP storage space as ISPs and web space providers charge by the megabyte. The more material you have stored, the more it costs you. Also, the longer it takes your customer to download it all, the more it costs them.

You may only need static HTML pages if your products or services do not vary much. However, you may require a database, payment and handling system, shopping baskets or a tracking system. Companies such as Actinic Software (www.actinic.co.uk) or Shop Creator (www.shopcreator.com) provide all these facilities in one product.

Organising the Content

The second step to web site development requires grouping all relevant information into sections sequentially and logically. This step should establish a basic design and identify which words or phrases should be used as the hyperlinks to connect the sections to each other. The web site might include the following:

- The main messages your company wants to convey about its business.

- The use of graphics, pictures or sounds to convey any messages or information.

- The separation of information into subgroups and pages.

- The labelling of each subgroup so that its heading clearly describes its contents.

- Each subgroup and page relating seamlessly with any others.

Planning the Layout

The third step requires planning how each section of the web site can be connected to each other section. The final layout should be left to the developer, but an initial site plan, or "story board", should be examined by those responsible for the business. For example, most developers fill the first pages of a web site with as much useful and relevant information, or added-value features, as possible, while always giving the visitor the option to purchase. Any in-depth or detailed information can be offered on a FAQ (frequently asked questions) page, with *the* most frequently asked questions listed first.

The following may help the development of *hierarchical* or *linear* format layouts:

- List the headings given to each of the subgroups on the web site's homepage (front page). This represents the web site *cover sheet* and its *table of contents.*

- The headings should be separate and arranged so that they show a logical sequence or progression from one to another.

- They should be organised to correspond to the cover sheet on the homepage, allowing users to move from section to section in sequence or jump from each section directly to the homepage. Section hyperlinks can also be represented by buttons: "start", "next page", and "previous page" etc.

Another format is the *freeform* layout format, which is useful when visitors to the site are expected to have different interests and information needs. It is also useful when the web site requires several distinct sections, such as company history, personnel information and descriptions of company products etc.

To develop the *outline* format, each of the separate sections used can be clustered into general subject categories. Each section needs a link to and from the homepage, and perhaps a "start" button, and words from the text then used to provide links to other sections. However, visitors should never be more than 2 to 3 clicks away from what they may be looking for.

It is possible to include links for all format layouts, as well as for other layouts within the same web site design. Although this is a complex project for developers, it is unlikely to confuse users because they would only see the hyperlinks, not the layouts which underpin them.

Online Catalogues

If you already produce a company catalogue, it should be put on your web site. This gives your customers the chance to browse it in their own time, without them waiting days for someone to post one to them. But that may not be enough. When people look through a catalogue, be it for clothes or scientific instruments, they do one of three things: they stop looking, they buy, or they continue the quest for more information.

Once they have browsed your online catalogue, they should be offered the option to be notified by e-mail of any updates to specific products. If they want more information, you should make it available. There is no point in making customers contact your company for more information because they may resent having to make the effort.

If you are going to invite people to do business with you over the Web you have to be fully prepared to handle all reasonable eventualities. You may need extra staff to maintain and update the site, to answer e-mail coming in from people visiting your home page, and you may need to get help from an agency in setting up and maintaining your site.

Choosing the Hyperlinks

Hyperlinks are the words, phrases or symbols within a document which serve as reference points or links to other parts of the same document or to other pages on the World Wide Web. It is these hyperlinks which give users the facility to move at will to any destination throughout the Web. Hyperlinks are the innovation the Internet was built around and its greatest asset.

It is due to hyperlinks that the Internet is a dynamic entity: if you do not include hot links to other pages on the Internet your company will not be taking full advantage of the Internet system. People who visit your web site page will not find it as useful if it has no links. Careful consideration should be made as to which links you want. Also, any URLs (uniform resource locators or web addresses) you want to highlight should be double-checked for accuracy.

Checking that Content is Legal

Confirm that your pages are legal. You can libel people, perform copyright infringements and other illegal acts if you are not careful. From a legal standpoint, web pages are publications similar to most media. Generally, any web site material should not be misleading or obscene. Also, make sure that all copyright in sites that may be created for you is assigned for you only. If you are unsure about the legality of any pages, get them checked by a lawyer before you publish them. There are lawyers on the Internet you can e-mail your pages to for that purpose (see Chapter 3, Small Business Opportunities on the Internet: Value-added Information Services: www.desktoplawyer.net).

Testing the Web Site's Functionality

The following suggestions may help to develop your web site's functionality and effectiveness:

- Ideally, your web pages should fit the computer monitor's screen, similar to a TV image, rather than requiring the user to scroll down each page. This design feature will become more important as we move towards Internet/TV integration (see Chapter 5: The Future of Internet Commerce: Internet-enhanced TV). To fit the average user's monitor, the screen resolution should be set to match that of the user's video card (55 per cent of cards are set to 800 x 600 resolution).[4]

- Your web site's URL should be included on every page, as users may print only one section of your web site.

- Remember the "2 to 3 click" rule: customers should never be more than three clicks away from what they are searching for. Also, every section of your web site should have a link back to its table of contents as some users may enter your site from a link on a different site.

- Design your web site so that those users whose software allows them to access text only can still benefit from the page.

- In addition to listing your company's e-mail address, an "e-mail us" hyperlink directly to your company should be included within your web site to encourage customer feedback and make it easier for customers to make contact with the company.

- Any content should have a uniform and consistent presentation style from section to section. This will simplify the web site navigation and convey a professional corporate image to customers.

- Your web site could include navigational buttons such as "next page", "previous page", "start", "contents page" (or "homepage") and "exit" in case users do not have software which enables them to control their movements while visiting a page.

- An index should be provided of all hyperlinks included within your web site which change colour or become highlighted after the sections that they refer to have been viewed.

- Your web site's hyperlinks, and all other facilities, should be tested using all of the popular Internet browsers. Your ISP should test these for you if they are providing you with the complete package of web page design, web space rental and so on.

- Your web site should be reviewed regularly to ensure that each of its links continues to work and is free of error messages, and that any links to other company's web sites continue to function properly and are correctly addressed.

Once your pages are checked, you can get them published by letting your ISP have the file. You can send the file by e-mail, on floppy disk, or by using FTP. FTP, the most popular method, involves you sending the file directly to the provider's computer without going through e-mail. Your ISP will give you details of what you need to do (see DIY Web Sites later in this chapter).

WEB SITE DEVELOPMENT

The most popular web site format is to have a series of pages describing and promoting what is to be sold, perhaps with a photo and a brief description, and a master index grouping products by price range etc. A search facility could be added to enable customers to choose all products in a given price range. Applications such as *QuickTime VR* may be used to produce user-driven interactivity, though the long download time and complexity of updating information may not be cost effective. At some point along this web site development chain, a decision has to be made when to stop adding new features and technologies. The key factor in this decision will invariably be money. Decisions may be based on rival firms' web sites in evaluating competitiveness.

Once the decision has been reached regarding what is to be put online you must next decide who is going to create this site. There are hundreds of web development agencies, and it is tempting to outsource the whole job and let them worry about hitting deadlines and sorting out CGI scripts etc.

If the work is outsourced, the development of the site should still have the company's input regarding specific, detailed site function. Each feature should be costed before being agreed to. A tight control of the site's budget should be exercised, making sure that estimates from several agencies are evaluated and that delivery dates are set with financial penalties if the company does not deliver on time. Checks should be made that the agency has enough staff and resources to deliver on its promises. Analysing the agency's portfolio and talking to its existing clients can help with this.

Outsourcing computing tasks of any kind has advantages: no day-to-day worries of code development and maintenance and no thinking about employing more staff. However, as the server hosting the web site will be located outside a small organisation, strict service levels should be defined. For example, allowable server problems and defining the time taken to update the site should be made clear. Financial penalties can be set for failing to deliver on these agreements. Outsourcing always presents the possibility of unnecessary charges or over-charging. As with most issues related to the problems of small businesses, what is really required is the advice and guidance of an honest broker.

If your business is a relatively high-tech company with its own expertise, it might be more cost effective to create your web site in-house. If the company does have the resources and ability to construct the site, provision should also be made to budget for upgrading and maintaining its appearance and content. Also, if the site is designed to provoke customer feedback, users will expect quick answers, so enough time should be allowed to manage responses. A compromise may be to hire a computer, or a part of a computer, on a service provider's network to host the site but have the development work done in-house.

If a site is run internally, experience, and probably staff, will be needed unless the owner-manager has the relevant skills. Employing staff may be a significant change in a small firm's strategy and should be evaluated thoroughly. Who is hired, on what terms and on what salary will have to be considered. For an estimate of what it costs to hire this kind of manpower, prospective employers can look up employment agencies such as www.pricejam.

co.uk. Equally important to an Internet strategy is the selection of hardware, software and networking technology needed for the job.

Good Design

Like any Internet page, a commercial web site needs to be attractive, well designed and easy for people to use. It should be a good place for customers to spend their time, browsing through the items you have for sale. Your company's homepage should include any mission statement you may want to include, as well as any re-assuring statements about your service, such as: information, privacy and data protection statements or delivery and payment promises.

Internet shop pages should have the following key items:

- Categories of products or services for sale

- Illustrations of products

- Prices

- Hot links to full descriptions (including illustrations) of products

- Methods of payment.

All the above elements should be represented in a clean, efficient and visually pleasing way. However, before deciding on the final design of your company's web pages you should visit the sites of other organisations that are likely to be nearer the cutting edge of web design. For example, Compaq (www.compaq.com), being a large computer retailer with a wealth of web development expertise, is an obvious site to visit. Similarly, The Graphics Company (see Case Studies: *The Graphics Company*), being a company concerned with good graphic design, also has a homepage that is an excellent example of clean design.

PLATE 9.2: COMPAQ

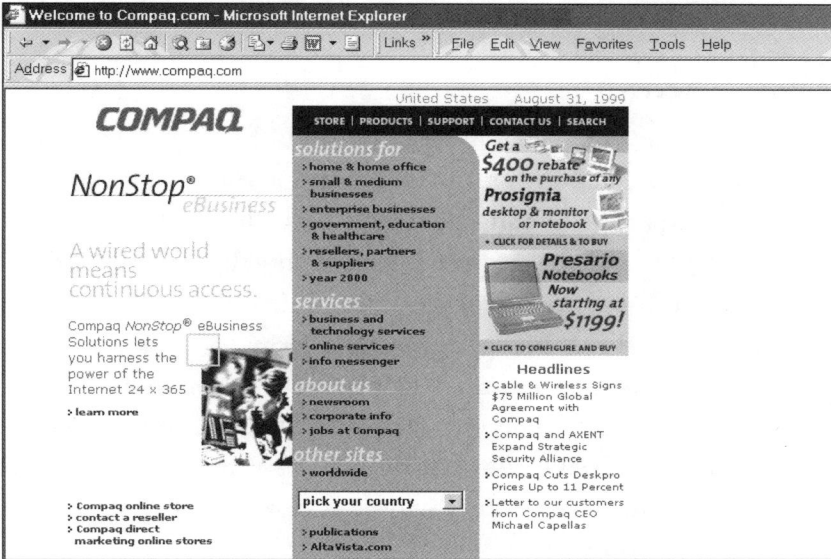

As is evident from the Compaq and The Graphics Company sites, in terms of web design, there is now a shift towards fast-downloading pages and easily navigated sites and away from multi-framed, multi-content sites with too many slow-appearing graphics. Although "roll-over" buttons, Java applets, Flash plug-ins and complex animations can be exceptionally clever and eye-catching, ultimately it will be its "user-friendliness" by which most visitors will judge your site.

Most web masters now recommend fast-downloading pages with tables, rather than frames, to align your content. Scrolling should be reduced to a minimum, with most of your site viewable within an area of 600 pixels wide and 400 pixels high so that it can be viewed on even the lowest screen resolution. A white or lightly coloured background is recommended, with darkly coloured text (so it is easily handled by printers), simple graphics and navigation buttons. This clean and efficient page design will also be more practical and easily viewed on the smaller mobile Internet-capable devices that are about to become commonplace in the near future (see Chapter 5, The Future of Internet Commerce: Mobiles).

Customer Access

Essentially, your web site's front page should give a clear indication of the exact categories of products and services you sell. Each of the individual items can have their own detailed page of description, which can be accessed from a hot link on the shop's front page. In this way, customers can go direct to the items they want to buy without being distracted. However, unlike a real shop, they will not be tempted to purchase other items as they look around. This can be overcome by a variety of other hot links that lead from the page selected by the customer to other pages that may be of interest. In this way you can attract customers to something else you may be selling.

ASSISTANCE SETTING UP A WEB SITE "SHOP FRONT"

There are a few ways a company can set-up a commercial web site online in partnership with others. A company can create a partnership with an Internet service provider. The ISP can set the web site up themselves or a consultant acting on their behalf. They will visit the organisation and develop the whole system, from page design to the fulfilment of orders. Alternatively, the company may only require the ISP or consultant to construct a virtual "shop front", while matters of stock control etc. may be managed in-house.

Working with an ISP provides a company with considerably more security than any other option. The ISP should have the experience not only to set up a web commerce site, but also to build a complete trading community. Such set-ups are sometimes called *extranets* or *Virtual Private Networks* (VPNs). This might be the easiest way to set up a web presence but there will be a premium to pay. Commission is paid on any credit card transactions, usually around two per cent, and any up-front costs may be in five figures, hardly within the budget of the smallest of businesses.

DIY WEB SITES

For small companies, using agencies may be too costly so the design has to be performed in-house. If this is the case for your company, make sure you get some design training first. Any company can construct an entire commercial Internet site itself. It can still make use of an ISP but the company becomes responsible for every aspect of its site. It can create the pages, link in the credit card payment schemes, make arrangements with the banks, glue the web site to any stock control and database systems and its customer care suite. For small businesses with limited budgets this may be the only option, but there are inherent dangers and costs.

There are various options for developing a business web site. ISPs may offer help lines, otherwise there are books, authoring programs, shareware or word processors to help design a web site. Books include *Easy Web Publishing with HTML .4*. Commercial web authoring programs including *Maximizer 5.0*, Claris *Web Site 3.0* or Adobe *PageMill 3.0*.[7] Less expensive web page builders such as IMSI's *Web Business Builder* do an adequate job.

Of the most popular web-editing programs the four main contenders are: Microsoft's *FrontPage 2000*, by far the most popular except with experts, SoftQuad's *HoTMetal PRO.5*, Allaire's *Home-Site.3* and Macromedia's *DreamWeaver.2*. *DreamWeaver* is the most popular program amongst professional web masters and comes with a copy of *HomeSite.4*, which is full of facilities that make the whole writing process easier. Both *Dream Weaver.2* and *FrontPage 2000* are visual editors, known as WYSIWYG ("what you see is what you get") letting the user work on a screen that looks as much as possible like the page will look in a browser. *Front Page*, however, takes away a lot of the control that experienced users demand. Word processors (e.g. Microsoft Word) have a "save as HTML" option that can also be used to convert text, though a separate FTP program may be needed to upload the pages online once the web site design is completed.

To build a web site with music, animation, video or dynamic graphics, rather than just static HTML pages, you will need to use "plug-ins" that are easily installed and used as part of your web site. According to Stat Market (www.statmarket.com), the five plug-ins most currently used on the Internet are: *Live Audio*, *Quick Time*, *AVI*, *Flash* and *Media Player*. *ActiveX* and *Java* can also be used to write small programs called "applets" that make it possible for a web page user to interact with the page.

Another option is to subscribe to a web site builder, for example, *ZyWeb Lite* (www.zy.com), which provides a step-by-step guide to building a web site.[8] Courses on Internet web page design are advertised in the Internet magazines. For newcomers to the Web, they may be essential.

Poor web page design is probably the number one reason why many pages do not get the readership the companies expect. Design should not be skimped on. Get it right at the outset and you will be rewarded with higher readership figures, higher visibility, cost effective marketing and a global corporate image you can be proud of.

PUBLISHING YOUR WEB PAGES

Once the design of your web site is completed, it becomes a collection of files stored on your hard disk. In order to create a web site that is on the Internet, you need to transfer these files on to your Internet server. If you are using an ISP for your web site you will need to transfer your files from your hard disk to your storage area on your ISP's computer using an FTP program. Free FTP programs can be downloaded from sites such as www.tucows.

com. Publishing your web pages can be done in the following way:

- Connect to your ISP.

- Run your chosen FTP program.

- Use the FTP dialogue boxes to connect to your storage area at your ISP and transfer your files from your hard disk to your ISP.

- Move or rename your files.

- Change the security on the files so that customers can read them.

- Leave the FTP program.

You will need to e-mail your ISP for the FTP addresses you should use to upload your files. Most ISPs will provide you with detailed instructions that show you exactly how to upload your files on their system. Once you have uploaded your web page files, anyone can view them by entering your web page URL into an Internet browser or search engine.

For companies that have an Internet server in-house, you only need to copy your web page files to this server. If you have effective security in place on your server, you might still have to use FTP to gain access to your own in-house server. Alternatively, if you are using an Internet server program that allows it, you may be able to copy the files over your office network.

CHECKLIST

- Register your domain name(s).

- Decide what your web site should be capable of (i.e. its functionality).

- Decide which payment methods you will require.

- Decide which delivery system you will require.

- Calculate all taxes and handling charges and include them in your web pages.

- Decide what your web site will look like.

- Organise the content.

- Plan the layout.

- Choose the hyperlinks.

- Check that the content will be legal.

- Decide what web design software your web site will require (e.g. FrontPage 2000, Dreamweaver.2, Flash.3, Fireworks.2, etc.).

- Test the web site's functionality.

- Decide whether any work should be outsourced or whether you will require extra staff.

References

[1] www.checkdomain.com

[2] www.domainnames.co.uk

[3] www.internic.net

[4] www.statmarket.com

[7] www.adobe.co.uk

[8] www.zy.com.

Part 3

Doing Business on the Internet

10

ATTRACTING AND KEEPING CUSTOMERS

All Internet surveys confirm that, currently, the Internet has a limited demographic range of potential customer. The typical Net user profile is English-speaking (60 per cent American), 84.5 per cent male, and 82.3 per cent white.[1] Users tend to be single, aged between 20 and 35, and 50 per cent have a degree. Thirty per cent of users have an income of over £40,000 (€62,000) and 55 per cent of users claim to use the Net for work, research and entertainment purposes. The EU audience tends to be even younger and is still made up of mostly students and the technically orientated.

Clearly, unless a company provides products or services for this specific target market audience then the chances of profitable commerce are minimal. It is essential that any Internet-based business should maintain ongoing consumer research to identify the specific, and changing, requirements of the Internet's limited market sector.

To adopt a market orientation, firms should attempt to understand their customers and identify the type of customer they want to attract. Building up customer databases can be a cost-effective means of collecting information about your customers. Monitoring relevant newsgroups may also help your business keep up to date with relevant developments and changes in public opinions and customer requirements. Information from other sources such as Internet-related journals and magazines may also provide useful sources of customer data.

Evidence suggests there are three types of customers: those looking to buy a specific item, "convenience shoppers" and "explorers" (those consumers who surf the Web looking for the best deal or most appropriate product combination).

Marketers must therefore reconstruct their advertising models for the new interactive, consumer-controlled, Internet medium to attract all three of these types of customers. The traditional customer loyalty ladder (Suspect, Prospect, Customer, Client, Partner, and Advocate) is still applicable, but now operates in a different fashion. The first three stages are often instantaneous in electronic commerce. The transition from customer to advocate relies on loyalty and is earned through buyer-seller relationships and consumer trust. The instantaneous nature of the Internet makes this more difficult (see Consumer Trust below).

For the time being, some companies may look at a web presence as one segment of the marketing mix.[2] Durlacher's *Quarterly Internet Report* recently revealed that whereas 33 per cent of all sizes of small and medium-sized enterprises (SMEs) in the UK and Ireland have a web site, few SMEs have yet to fully embrace electronic commerce.[3] Presently, most small firms see a web presence as another advertising medium rather than a significant environment for commerce.

A major problem for businesses trying to promote their products and services is making customers aware of their web presence. Without highly visible and expensive marketing, which most small firms cannot afford, their web sites may remain invisible unless they use all marketing opportunities intelligently.

To become an Internet-based company you should find out as much as possible about your potential customers — what they want, how they perceive your company, and what proportion of your overall customer base use the Internet. It is important to evaluate how many of those customers who use the Internet would deal with a company directly over the Net rather than use traditional methods. Finding out this kind of information at the outset of any Internet venture is vital. It is no good setting up an Internet presence if your customers do not use it.

REACHING CUSTOMERS

Your company needs to gather information on how it might reach new customers. You should also find out how much it costs to advertise, produce direct mail leaflets, and use the Internet. Most Internet magazines include tables of advertising costs from the leading ISPs in Europe. A company should decide which customers it wants to target, and with which specific products and services, and decide how it is going to reach and to sell directly to them. A definitive marketing plan should be devised to target all the requirements necessary for the company to achieve its strategic objectives.

Make sure that you also advertise your web site through any relevant non-Internet media. For example, you could send a press release to any trade magazines that cover your industry telling them that your company is now running on the Web. It is also worth sending details of your new web site to the many Internet magazines published each month. These computer magazines normally carry "what is new" and "best site" features, and might include your site if it is interesting.

Once you have announced your web site to the press, together with your full URL and an e-mail address, as many people as possible should be informed about your web presence. You should have stationery reprinted with details of e-mail and web page addresses. Publish your web site address widely: on headed paper, business cards, leaflets, adverts, brochures and so on. You should also check your company's search engine ranking. The best site to check that your web site has been ranked successfully on search engines and directories is Search Engine Watch (www.searchenginewatch.com).

GETTING LISTED

At present, the most reliable and cost effective option for getting
your web site advertised online is to get it listed in as many search
engines and directory indexes as possible and then to update
these listings regularly with new features.

There are two ways of registering your web site with a search
engine: you can visit the search engine directly and manually fill
out an electronic registration form, or you can use an automated
program to do this work for you across all the search engines.
Visiting each search engine yourself takes time but allows you to
enter exactly the information you want to appear on the search
index. If you use an automated program to do the work, it will
ask you once for short and long descriptions of your site and
submit these to the search engines. You cannot then alter the information to each index, but it does save time.

Automated registration programs normally provide a free
service in which your site's details are sent to a dozen of the top
search engines. If you want the registration program to send the
information to every search engine on the Internet then you may
have to pay for this. However, it may well be worth the costs to
ensure that your site is on each index.

Some of the main registration companies are Add Me
(www.addme.com), Exploit (www.exploit.com) and Submit It!
(www.submit.com). For example, Submit It! currently offers to list
a site in 30 different web sites and search engine indexes without
charge for a trial period. Alternatively, companies can visit Exploit (see Plate 10.1) and download the *Submissions Wizard*. This is
now available for Windows 95, Windows 98, and Macintosh, and
can automate submission to dozens of search engine sites. Exploit
can also process a firm's application to reverse-engineer the software used by the search engines to make sure your site appears
towards the top of any search result list. Some search engines list
companies in alphabetical order. According to research, the nearer
the top of the search list a firm appears the more likely the aver-

age consumer is to use it.[4] Currently, Add Me can list your company in 30 directories for free, including all the most popular search engines. Companies should also visit any local directory sites or country-specific search engines to register their URL.

PLATE 10.1: EXPLOIT.COM

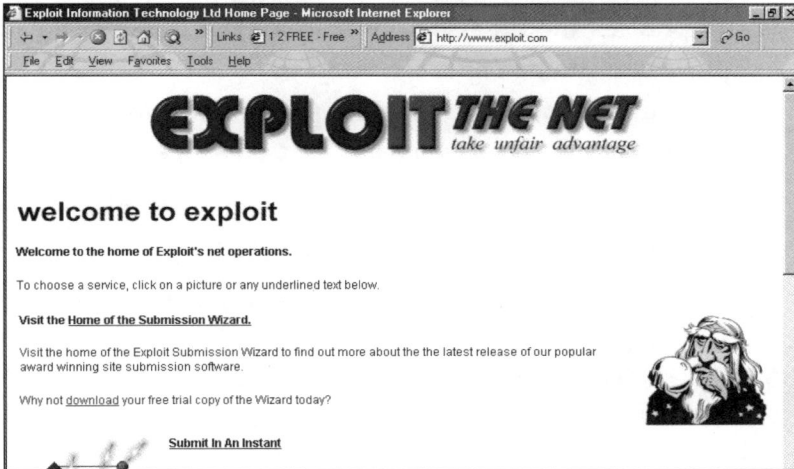

Another way to gain immediate attention from search engine users is to buy advertising space in the opening pages of a search engine's index, but this can be an expensive option (e.g. it costs £23,560 every two weeks for inclusion on the home page of Yahoo!*). Also, because this kind of service is so new, it is difficult to evaluate what kind of return there is for this considerable fee.

Improving your Search Engine Listing

It is a great advantage for any company to appear near the top of a search list, as potential customers are statistically more likely to choose the first relevant company they find. Therefore, any technique that can help achieve a higher search listing should be considered.

---

* Correct at time of going to press.

Many popular search engines work by searching for, and matching, key words and phrases that users type into the search engine's dialogue box. Therefore, it can help your company's search engine listing to include *meta tags* in your home page's HTML code that match the keywords and phrases users are likely to use when looking for subjects relevant to your site. These key words and phrases should also appear in the bar of your site and in the copy of your home page.

There are several meta tags, but the most important for search engine indexing are the *description* and *key words* tags:

• Description tags return a description of a page in place of the summary a search engine would ordinarily create.

• Key word tags provide key words for the search engine to associate with a page.

These meta tags should be placed inside the header tags in the following way:

<HEAD>

<TITLE>Your company </TITLE>

<META name = "description" content = "Every popular computer game at the lowest prices.">

<META name = "keywords" content = "computer games, computer, games, prices, latest releases, Sony, Nintendo, Sega">

</HEAD>

In the search engines that support description tags, your web site listing will appear like this:

Your company
Every popular computer game at the lowest prices.

This technique will help the description match what is in the description tag. The key word tag also provides the chance of a potential customer typing in "computer games" or perhaps "Nintendo" + "games" and having that search criteria matched with your page.

It should be taken into account that tags are becoming less relevant to search engine enquiries. Increasingly, search engines and directories are becoming more sophisticated and diversified in their search criteria. Search facilities are moving towards prioritisation such as site popularity, links to other related sites and, more commonly, relevant descriptive text within site pages. Therefore, meta tags are now mainly used as an additional design element and should be used in conjunction with descriptive text and relevant links on your initial web pages.

SEARCH ENGINES AND DIRECTORIES

Any company on the Net should research which search engines and directories are most likely to be used by their target market. If search engine organisers charge fees for including your home page in their index, you should make the following enquiries:

- If the index specialises in any particular subject

- The most frequently visited subjects or categories

- If the index is a commercial one

- How frequently the index is updated.

PUBLICISING A WEB SITE

Once your web site is designed and tested, you have received space at your ISP, and have been allocated a URL, you should then plan your publicity campaign. To publicise your site the following should be contacted:

- All search engines and directories

- All the page owners you have hot links to

- All customers

- All suppliers.

Be certain to let every search engine on the Internet know of your existence by sending them details of your URL. Each search engine web site has a facility (usually a button) to do this. When the search engines list all the details of your web site, anyone in the world making a search could then find your web site. Your URL should also be added to all printed materials, advertising and e-mails as a signature file (see Chapter 11, Advertising and Marketing on the Internet: Signature Files).

GENERATING WEB SITE TRAFFIC

Once your web site has been built, and the advertising strategy is in place, the company has to let the potential customer know about it. For a commercial site the number of *hits* is the yardstick by which, presently, success is judged. A "hit" is a request processed by the server. If a company has a page with graphics, every time a visitor loads the page each graphic will register as a separate hit. One person can generate hundreds of hits every time they visit.

It is important for any Internet-based business to know exactly how many people are visiting, and there are a number of ways to do this. Your ISP should be able to supply a company with a *log* recording the number of visitors. That log may also tell the company how many separate in-coming IP addresses were recorded, though this may not be accurate. Visitors accessing via AOL, for example, may all have the same IP address.

A more reliable course of action is for a company to set up its own counter on a particular page to gauge activity on its web site. A counter can be either visible or invisible to site visitors, and is simply a piece of HTML code, which calls up a graphic from an external site. There may be two counters on a web site, e.g. one on the main homepage and one on the contents page, and both may be made invisible to visitors. Every time the page is loaded the counter sends a trigger to the external web site, and each of these is recorded. At any time this site can be visited and checked to see how many people are visiting the site. Several companies offer counter services for web developers, or counters can be created in-house using a program called CGI (see Data Publishing later in this chapter).

Drawing visitors to a site initially is important, but it is equally important to make sure they come back. The most effective strategy for generating user traffic to a site is similar to those of good advertising strategies: a business should identify its target market and what they want. The site should be simple, include timely information, and be constantly updated. It should also be attractive and easily navigated. Each web page should also be kept small (less than 30Kb) to ensure the site is fast to download. If there is real depth of content potential customers will value the site and bookmark it. A business should keep in touch with its visitors through feedback and respond to that feedback. A simple feedback form can be created on the site to record visitor details.

Your company should also consider developing a global strategy as visitors may be from all over the world, so building a culturally neutral environment to a web site may provide a competitive advantage with few extra costs. If a company wants a free global launch they could hold it on IRC (Internet Relay Chat: www.irc.com). IRC provide a forum which allows simple conferencing (one-to-many conversations). IRC offers several means to achieve this: to a list, to a group (channel) or one-to-all.

The one-to-all type of message is best described as a "broadcast" message. A single broadcast message can result in a huge response from the intended recipients. A company can set up their own channel and invite everybody to log on at a certain time to meet each other. A company can also promote its party in newsgroups and on its site (see Plate 10.2).

PLATE 10.2: SAMPLE IRC

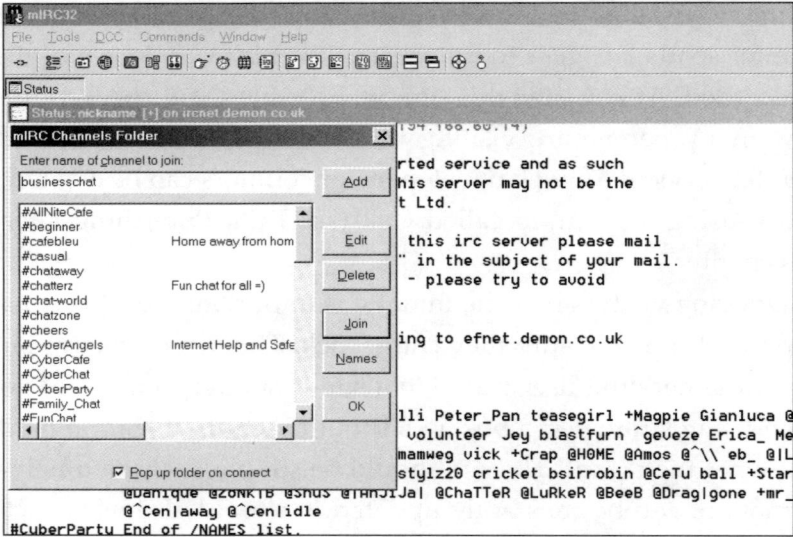

Thought should be given as to your company's domain name and how easy it is to remember. It is the *brand* by which your company's site will be known, and in Internet marketing the brand is vital. Names should not be flash, or use any unusual spellings or include any words that are spelt differently in America. If your company's budget allows, registration of a few versions of a domain may prove profitable, as it may appeal to a slightly wider audience. Companies can register their web site with Emap's *What's New* site at www.emap.com/whatsnew. By doing this your company can be listed in what is currently the fastest growing new site directory in the world.

Most potential customers tend to find a site through search engines, such as Lycos, Yahoo! and Alta Vista. Your company can register its URL with each of these, by visiting their sites and following the instructions onscreen (see Getting Listed). For example, Lycos alone has estimated that it has currently indexed more than one million URLs.

Usenet newsgroups are an excellent source of web site visitors. Lists of groups relevant to company sites can be accessed here and companies can subscribe to them. Businesses can then post a message to "visit our new web site". A record should be made of people posting messages, which could directly relate to your company's site. Your company can then reply to the group and point out if more information is available at another URL.

SEX SELLS

The following are *not* Internet sex sites:

- www.finger.com

- www.fist.com

- www.gobble.com

- www.phuck.com

- www.pierce.com

- www.pluckit.com

- www.sade.com

- www.spank.com.

All the above URLs are in fact Internet-related companies such as web designers, software houses or domain name registration companies. The reason that so many Internet-related companies use sexually-oriented domain names is because of the fact that up to 80 per cent of all Internet enquiries are for pornography (see Appendix 5c). As most Internet users conduct web searches by typing in key words into a search engine, and most of those searches are for pornography, the use of a sexually explicit word for a domain name increases immensely the chances of a potential customer accidentally accessing a company's web site.

This marketing device is currently the most effective way for an Internet-based business to create "passing trade". Just as in the real world, in cyberspace a business can make sales from "impulse" buying; a customer accidentally comes across something they like when looking for something else. An example of this very real Internet phenomena is the confectioners Sweet Seduction.[5] Since going online in 1995 the company has more than 1,000 hits each week, selling over £1,000 worth of chocolates. Very few of these orders were from customers who were originally looking for a sweet shop!

Using Newsgroups to Attract Customers

The Usenet on the Internet is a collection of individual discussion groups called newsgroups. There are currently over 16,000 different newsgroups covering just about every subject you can imagine. To market your site effectively, you should look in the newsgroups that concern your product range or service provision and read the submissions.

Anyone can "post" a message to a newsgroup, either to reply to a previous message or to start a new subject. You should not send messages to every newsgroup with a long advert about your company, as this advertising device (called "spamming") is not acceptable "netiquette". The newsgroups should be used with respect. The best strategy is to follow the discussions and then start to add your own views or suggest your site for further information. There is a guide to all the newsgroups at www.dejanews. com. If you cannot find a newsgroup that covers your specific subject area, you can set-up your own newsgroup through your ISP.

Customer Service

Once customers have been attracted to your company's web site, they then have to be encouraged to visit your site consistently. Customer service is among the best customer-retention investments any organisation can make. Customer service is an all-embracing term, which covers those added extras which are not part of the actual product or service being sold: efficiency, on-time delivery, and cost-effectiveness are some of the main components of customer service. For example, late delivery is one of the most frequent causes of customers' complaints.

The more help a company provides, which is not asked for or charged for, the more likely that company is to receive continued support and repeat orders. Customers are also likely to recommend that business to others — a very valuable means of attracting new custom. The value of "word of mouth" advertising on the Internet should not be underestimated, especially considering the increasing number of newsgroups, chat-rooms, and talk shops on the Net.

The sort of added extras a company can provide as part of a customer service package will depend on the sort of business it operates, but the following are some ideas to consider:

- Free delivery.

- Free telephone advice on use of product in the period immediately after purchase.

- Free training, or training literature, in the use of a product.

- Free promotional merchandise (e.g. mouse mats and t-shirts) with initial orders.

- Extended guarantee of products for a nominal fee.

- Reduced prices on further orders after the first purchase.

- Three items for the price of two offers, etc.

Many companies now issue a *Statement of Customer Service*. If a company produces its own web site customer service plan it will be more likely to attract repeat orders, since purchasers will know that they will benefit from more than just a product or service.

CONSUMER TRUST

"People should get what they pay for online, and it should be easy to get redress if they don't. We must give consumers the same protection in our virtual mall that they now get at the shopping mall." (Bill Clinton, 1998)[1]

Creating consumer trust is a major issue in electronic commerce and especially Internet commerce. If the consumer does not trust the seller then commerce will not take place. This fact represents a big risk of not acquiring, or worse, losing consumer trust. When the buyer operates in the conventional markets they can quite often check the goods before buying and they can even check the company by entering the premises. If the transaction is made in local markets both parties are aware of the legislation regulating the rights of the buyer and seller.

However, when a consumer acts over country boundaries, there can be some problems as most countries do not have consumer protection legislation. Taxing is a similarly difficult barrier to Internet trade. When we think about a net transaction; the client may be in one country, the seller in another, and logistics may deliver the goods from a third. The concern of the customer may be as to where these taxes should be paid and which country's law applies (see Chapter 12, Electronic Payments: Taxation).

Privacy

Privacy is a key aspect of consumer trust, though what is regarded as private may differ from one person to another as well as between different cultures. Those who currently use the Internet may be better-educated and therefore less willing to give information, unless they trust the recipient (see Appendix 1). Companies need to realise that the only reason they should hold information on a customer is because they have a relationship with that customer; something which is not transferable. Those using electronic channels to reach customers are likely to target better-educated and more affluent customers. They need, therefore, to ensure that their customer information systems are appropriate.

An understanding of the trust-building process is also required. Trust is best developed through processes. Processes tend to be customer-facing; within each customer interaction trust is either built-up or eroded. Companies must be absolutely clear about the value and intended use of information. Collecting information simply because it is technically possible, or one day might be useful, is likely to weaken trust-development.

For example, if you run a competition on your site, or request visitors to register, and then transfer that data to a server in a country without a similar level of data protection as the EU, then you are contravening EU data protection laws. Also, if you were then to sell that data, or any personal information concerning those people, without acquiring their permission, then you would also be contravening EU laws.

Whilst there is much discussion on the issues of Internet privacy and security, in the context of normal business activities, many millions of people trust others with their personal financial information. Examples include ordering over the telephone, passing a credit card to an unknown waiter, and even signing direct debit mandates. If an error occurs in these types of transactions we trust the service provider to correct the error. However, this trust has been nurtured over a time-span the Internet cannot yet match.

Data Protection Registrar

In the UK, if a company is going to use a computer in its business, and expects to keep any kind of information about other people on it, such as an address list, it is required by law to register with the Data Protection Registrar (www.dpr.gov.uk). This puts the business on a central register of people who have information relating to individuals on their computers. Normally this registration would last three years. EU data protection laws determine that all European companies within member states should now register with their own country's data registrar if they are to keep customer records on databases.

Authentication

Authentication is another problem in terms of consumer trust. If a trustworthy business partner cannot be authenticated the risk of participating in criminal or fraudulent actions is high. There are not many methods for verifying that the other party on the Net is who or what they claim to be.

The naming system in the Internet is quite vulnerable and depends on name servers hosted by Internet services or access providers. These servers are man-made software products that may be hacked to give false information to lead customers to a fake site. Another risk point is the human naming convention; if a brand name is easily misspelled somebody might put up a fake electric point of sale with the typo name of a real site. Authentication is also necessary to avoid totally fraudulent actors setting up a look-a-like electronic commerce site with no intention of delivering any order of pre-paid products.

Because Internet consumers may not know anything of the Internet retailers they are dealing with, they need a third party to create the trust. Three kinds of organisations can act as trust creators: banks, electronic malls, and certification organisations. For example, a bank's role is to act as a regulator; banks can easily stop payment transfers and that should mean the end of fraudulent transactions.

Barclays Bank has joined a banking consortium that will issue unique digital identities, called "certificates", to ensure secure Internet trading. Barclays has joined eight banks and e-commerce security seller CertCo to issue certificates and boost business-to-business e-commerce. Certificates provide certainty of trading partners' identities when trading across the Internet. Each of the banks will issue digital certificates to participating corporations and their employees. Using certificates, traders can identify other users of the system.

Participating in an e-mall may be more secure for your small business than building your own site. The mall is a facilitator; it collects a set of retailers together to attract more consumers to one-stop shopping, like physical malls. Because the mall gets its money from business done by independent sellers, the mall has every reason to keep the site clean. Bank's regulating actions may even stop the whole mall if an independent company using the mall's payment facility begins to act suspiciously.

Legislation

Things may differ in the virtual world, and the consumer may feel that the Internet has yet to prove it has total security for retailer-consumer transactions. However, in the EU we do have a working legislation in place to regulate commerce. If the transactions are made via electronic information exchange it does not affect any statutory rights of the consumer. The problem arises when the consumer knows nothing of the other party, where it resides, and whether it actually exists.

For a trustworthy company to gain consumer trust it should be remembered that the name of its web site might be the only thing the customer knows. That is the reason why several companies and organisations build their web site names from their company names (e.g. www.cocacola.com, www.visa.com, www.ibm.com) or use their brand names (e.g. www.budweiser.com, www.rayban.com). Some Internet-based companies use local contact points to give consumers a feeling of the company's physical presence. This may be a good idea if all claims and problems can be solved there. Legislation in most EU countries approves a maximum of two domain names per company and regulates heavily the names to be derived from the company's official name.

The Internet Consumers Assistance Bureau (ICAB)[2] has been formed to prevent consumers from falling foul of potential Internet fraud. ICAB retains records of companies trading on the Net and may warn consumers if a particular firm has a dubious reputation. Also if a consumer requires information regarding the actual geographic base of a company, a potential issue with the global nature of the Internet, ICAB has the facilities to find out.[3]

The European Commission has proposed a Directive that would bring e-commerce into line with the Single Market. If the proposal becomes an EU Directive, it will force individual member states to implement the Directive in national law. It defines the "place of establishment" of a business as "the place where an operator actually pursues an economic activity through a fixed establishment, irrespective of where web sites or servers are situated." This would prevent businesses setting up servers overseas so as to bypass local laws. The Directive would also require businesses "to make available to customers basic information concerning their activities", including an e-mail address, trade registration number and VAT number.

VALUE-ADDED SELLING

Many companies use information to promote their products, and present this as an additional customer service. Such promotions are called *infomercials,* and at their best are blends of interesting, relevant facts along with a sales pitch for the company's particular products. Through this highly skilled use of information, companies draw new business while also adding value to the customers' shopping experience. The Internet enables businesses to provide similar informercial services, but at considerably lower cost. The information a business offers works like an incentive gift and can build strong relationships with customers. The goodwill this fosters is of enormous benefit to word-of-mouth sales and reputation enhancement.

Value-added selling differs markedly from traditional advertising as the latter sends a single, unchanging message to a wide audience, while the former provides extensive information to a select group that can choose for themselves what information they need. Advertising on its own uses single messages, is a limited format, targets its audience, and controls presentation. Value-added selling should be information rich, have a multimedia format, contain a user-led search format, and invite user feedback.

Value-added selling can also offer a simultaneous blend of entertainment and education so that it attracts buyers by giving them novelty features and games while also maintaining their interest with useful information about products. Furthermore, unlike traditional media advertising, the Internet is forgiving. Unsuccessful promotions can be discarded or changed daily at minimum cost, and customer feedback can be used to improve presentations.

The main challenge for Internet sellers is to discover what kind of information their customers want and value. A business should analyse how it usually promotes its products; through word of mouth, printed advertisements, or perhaps incentive gifts etc. A company should evaluate those promotional activities that are effective and eliminate those that are ineffective.

To add value to its product or service, a company should also evaluate whether ineffective features could be improved if customers were given more information, and what that information could be. For example, when developing a product or service, the data gathered as a matter of routine may also be of interest to customers. Questionnaires or fact sheets can be used effectively to summarise and explain products, services, and special features. Product information should be presented so that current users are interested enough to pass promotional information on to other target groups.

One of the benefits of the Internet is that it contains millions of files with programs, documents and databases. Useful or interesting files could be stored on your web site for visitors to download. To include shareware files on your web site, check with the author to make sure that he or she does not object.

DATA PUBLISHING

Statistics show that most Internet users are in search of information. To allow a visitor to search for information on your web site you may need to use the Perl programming language to create scripts that run on the Internet server. If you are using an ISP to host your web site, then this solution is really the only one available to allow visitors to search for information on your site.

The system works as follows: save your data either in separate files for each item (useful if you have just a few dozen items with lots of text) or save your data as separate lines in a few large files (which is useful if you have lots of small items of text). For example, if you want to provide a database of products together with a description and prices, you might put the details of each product into a different file. However, if you have a simple dictionary or glossary, you might store each word and definition on a separate line of a single large file.

These data files (which would normally be just plain text files or HTML formatted files) are stored in a separate folder with your main web site page files on your ISP's computer. You would transfer the files on to the remote computer, using FTP. To allow a visitor to search any of these data files you will need two more items: a web page with a form that lets the user enter a search term and a script that will actually search through each word in each file to find a match.

To write a script that can carry out these functions is not easy. You should either contact your ISP who might already have a library of scripts written ready for you to use, or you will need to hire a programmer to do the work for you. The programming language most often used to write scripts is called Pen and the system of connecting your web page to the script is called CGI. If you search the Web (e.g. using www.yahoo.com) for CGI tutorials you will get a good grounding in the language.

PUBLISHING DOCUMENTS ON THE INTERNET

Rather than letting visitors search through a database, you might want to publish a text, such as a monthly journal or company report, directly on the Internet. You could create a web page that contains all the text of this document, limiting access to this web page using password access. An alternative is to store a document file on the web server and allow users to download the document file to read on their word processor or to use a viewer such as Adobe Acrobat.

If you want to publish a document text on the Internet you will need to create the file and save it to the ISP's computer where you store your web pages. You could then include a link to the file within a web page, allowing visitors to download the file using FTP. Alternately, you could password protect the file and ask for payment and registration.

OFFERING SUPPORT

If you want to maintain a good reputation, promote your company and your products and services, you should offer customer support (globally) if you are to sell them across the Internet. Indeed, this may well be a legal requirement in certain countries to which you sell.

For most companies, international support should not be a problem. You can provide telephone help lines, customer support pages on the Internet, and so on. For businesses that are product-orientated, servicing internationally may be more difficult, unless you are already an established worldwide business. However, do not neglect planning for customer service delivery, as this business element alone could determine your sales success on the Internet.

DISCOUNTS

Lower prices is consistently quoted by Internet users as one of the main reasons for shopping online. Companies can offer these price reductions due to the reduced cost of overheads the Internet provides. Internet-based companies like Amazon.com have achieved their phenomenal success largely through offering popular items (e.g. books and compact disks) at heavily discounted prices. The same can be said of online companies offering travel, tickets and other items. Discounts, therefore, can be an excellent way of attracting custom.

However, discounts should not be offered to anyone and everyone; they must bring in some advantage to a business. If a company gets nothing in return for a discount it is effectively giving its customers money. This will reduce profits and do the business no good at all.

Discounts could be offered for customers who buy more than a specified number of items. Bulk-buying discounts encourage customers to buy larger amounts of goods to reduce the unit cost; this increases a company's volume of business and so adds to its profits. However, the bulk discount level should not be set so low that everyone qualifies. Otherwise it will only lower the company's overall income. The discount level should be just low enough to encourage a fair proportion of customers to make larger orders and so increase overall income.

The golden rule of pricing is to charge the maximum price customers are prepared to pay and get them to pay quickly. To follow this rule, a company will need to know the following:

- The prices of any competitive companies

- The cost and profit margins required.

These two factors can be used to calculate prices. If customers are prepared to pay that price, a company should not change it. If customers are not prepared to pay that price for a company's product or service, the costs should be reviewed and reduced if possible, without reducing profit margins.

GUARANTEES

If a company *can* support its product(s) with a guarantee, it should be emphasised on the company's web site and sales literature. This will help increase the professional image of the company and improve the confidence of any prospective purchaser. The fact that a company agrees to repair or replace any faults mentioned in its guarantee means that its level of customer service, and customer confidence, will be higher than competitors who do not offer guarantees and so increases the chances of attracting and keeping customers.

RETAINING CUSTOMERS

Statistics prove that customers either visit a site once and never return, or visit the same sites repeatedly.[6] An average visitor to any site will only make two or three clicks to find what they want before leaving that site. Easy navigation, fast loading and clear pathways to facilities such as product information or purchase order forms are essential. Your site should use plain language in a polite manner. Customer participation and personal information should be encouraged but never insisted upon. Any commercial web site should be a fun and up-to-date environment.

Your aim should be to identify new customers and your best customers. Then you should use customer purchase history to personalise any communications or dialogue with customers. When a purchase is made, try to reinforce the customer's satisfaction in their decision by congratulating them on their choice of purchase. You may also suggest other related or complimentary products or services they may be interested in. Lastly, thank them for their custom. The more a customer feels comfortable and "involved" in your site, the more likely you are to retain their custom. Remember the 80/20 retail principle that 20 per cent of customers represent 80 per cent of profit; it is cheaper to retain customers than it is to attract new ones.

CHECKLIST

- Get your web site address listed in as many search engines and directory indexes as possible.

- Add your web site and e-mail addresses to all printed materials.

- Target a specific customer profile you know uses the Internet.

- Keep in touch with visitors through feedback and respond to that feedback.

- Add a feedback form to your web site to record visitor details.

- Use a *log* recording the number of visitors to your web site.

- Attempt to build buyer-seller relationships and consumer trust.

- Build a customer database.

- Identify new customers and your best customers.

- Use customer purchase history to personalise communications with customers.

- Keep up-to-date with online customer trends.

- Use the Usenet newsgroups to help promote commerce.

- Issue a *Statement of Customer Service* and offer customer support.

- Use value-added selling techniques offering information and/or entertainment.

- Evaluate those promotional activities that are effective and those that are not.

- Offer discounts to customers who buy more than a specified number of items.

- Give accurate prices and realistic delivery times.

- Try to support your product(s) with a guarantee.

- Ensure that visitors are only two or three clicks away from what they are looking for.

- Use fast links to product information or purchase order forms.

- Encourage customer participation and personal information.

- Always try to make the customer feel comfortable and "involved" in your site.

- When a purchase is made, try to reinforce the customer's satisfaction in their decision by congratulating them on their choice of purchase.

- Suggest other complimentary products or services they may be interested in.

- Thank customers for their custom.

References

[1] The Net, BBC 2, 2 February 1998

[2] Dibb, D. Lyndon, S. Williams, M.P. & Ferrell, O.C. *Marketing: Concepts and Strategies* (Houghton Mifflin Co.: London) 1991, p. 20

[3] *Financial Mail on Sunday*, 30 August 1998, p. 28

[4] *Internet Magazine*, (Cradley Print: UK), July 1998, p. 115

[5] http://connexion.parallax.co.uk/seduct/.

---

[6] OECD: *Dismantling the Barriers to Global Electronic Commerce.* http://www.oecd.
org/sti/it/ec/prod/dismantl.htm

[7] www.isitsafe.com

[8] *Computer Act!ve Magazine,* 27 August 1998, p. 10

[9] www.statmarket.com.

11

ADVERTISING AND MARKETING ON THE INTERNET

MARKETING A BUSINESS ON THE INTERNET

For most businesses, the Internet presents an excellent opportunity for global marketing. You can let anyone in the world who has Internet access know of your existence. At the end of June 1999 there was a global online population of approximately 159 million and the number grows by tens of thousands every day.[1]

By all appearances, the Web is a marketer's dream: presently, no other medium allows advertisers to interact directly with their customers. Yet despite its potential, web advertising can be a frustrating experience for advertisers and content providers. Similar to other web-related developments, online advertising is currently still to realise its own expectations due, mostly, to the small cross-section of consumers presently online. However, provided your company has the correct strategic fit for e-commerce and uses Internet marketing intelligently, the potential for generating huge profits is undeniable.

Online advertisers usually pay a site-rate based on every thousand times their ad is seen. Online advertising is markedly more expensive per impression — double or even triple the cost of advertising in print, television or radio. Online advertising is also very hard to evaluate in terms of cost and return. For example, *ad tracking* can accurately measure how many people click on a banner ad but cannot effectively track whether such hits result in viable sales leads. Online retailers can now evaluate their advertising costs, but the marketing management software required for cost/benefit ratio calculations is very expensive.

Without a reliable way to relate hits to consumer purchases, online marketing companies cannot be held accountable for how many sales leads they generate. If no one can tell whether a banner ad results in worthwhile sales leads, not to mention actual online transactions, advertisers cannot evaluate the effectiveness of any online marketing campaign. Potential Internet advertisers cannot accurately evaluate why an ad may have a low hit rate. It may be, for example, because the web site is unattractive or because the content site, where the banner appears, does not target an audience fitting known Net demographics.

Another problem is a lack of auditing standards across sites. Without uniform metrics and definitions most marketing agencies evaluate an advertisement by its "hit rate" to determine an advertisement's effectiveness. Until standards are agreed upon, information from reports evaluating across sites will remain fundamentally flawed, useful only for short-range plans and short-term campaigns. The Web is an exciting new advertising medium and, as such, requires a new way of thinking.

In order for the Internet to live up to its potential, advertisers need to stop emphasising how many times a banner ad is flashed before viewers. While auditing standards do not guarantee accurate information regarding the amount of hits, standards at least will provide advertisers with a baseline from which they can measure their campaigns across multiple sites. Direct marketers, advertisers and content sites are starting to demand more advanced technologies that will enable the kind of tracking and targeting the Web promises.

The Web is interactive. Therefore, Internet advertisers should target their efforts towards developing an interactive buyer-seller relationship based on inducements, added-value content and customer feedback.

PROMOTIONAL DEVICES

Press releases, magazines surveys and evaluations, local radio and press advertising, e-mail marketing and customer reviews can all help to promote your commercial web site. Your company may decide to buy promotional give-aways to engage key contacts and customers. Small or cheap promotional gifts such as mouse mats, t-shirts, and post cards, etc. with the company logo on them may be a good idea, as this will help to reinforce customer loyalty (an integral part of e-commerce) and promote the company's brand. This practice gains or enforces competitive advantage through brand recognition.

Most successful web development companies suggest that free downloads are an excellent promotional device; a simple screen-saver has proved to be one of the most popular free gifts. With so much shareware on the Web, companies can contact authors and request to copy their software to their site and make it available for download.

Competitions are also efficient customer attractions. There are lots of competitions on the most popular web sites, which are promoted in newsgroups and mailing lists. Increased profits are not the only reason to initiate e-commerce; increasing market share by selling "loss leader" products over the Net may generate non-Net-related revenues later on. The Net can also be used to build up a new presence in a particular market sector.

To optimise the accuracy of target marketing the Internet can be used for market research by surveying Internet users. One of the most powerfully compelling things about the Internet is that it allows companies direct and real-time access to its customers. Market research usually takes months, and may cost a great deal, but may now be carried out much more quickly and cost-effectively online. It is possible to conduct various types of research online (see Chapter 14, Research on the Internet).

SIGNATURE FILES

A signature file is a small piece of text added to the bottom of every e-mail message and newsgroup posting sent. Almost every electronic mail program lets you create a corporate signature file, usually by clicking "add signature" on a dialogue box. They normally consist of a few lines of text with your company name, company logo or slogan, and contact details. The signature file is added automatically to the end of any e-mail message you send and provides a good company advert.

Organisations should use their signature file wisely. It should include the company's URL and a short description of their site. Any potential customers curious to find out more about the company may then easily visit the site. You should also create a similar signature file to use with your newsgroup browser so that it will automatically add your contact details to any message you post to a newsgroup. In a newsgroup, thousands of potential visitors may read a company's message.

LINKS TO RELATED SITES

Try and get a link to your web site added to other sites that cover similar subjects. Find the sites that you think might attract similar visitors and mail the host with your request. Also suggest that you add a link back to their site in return. This will provide visitors to either site with a quick way to visit related sites. If you build up enough related links you might soon find that visitors visit your web site for this reason alone, as a provider of useful links.

SWAP BANNER ADVERTISING

Your firm may gain competitive advantage through joining schemes such as *The Internet Link Exchange* (www.linkexchange. com). The idea is that your company includes banners advertising other companies on your site. For every two banners you display, your own banner is displayed somewhere else on the Web. It is free to join, and there are companies who will create a banner for participating companies. Your company can also carry sponsorship banners on your site (see Chapter 3, Small Business Opportunities on the Internet: Sponsorships).

Not only does this marketing technique generate free advertising for your company's site, but it also provides a source of statistics. Your company can keep track of how many banners you have displayed, how many times your banner has appeared, and how many people have visited your site because of it. This free use of advertising banners and links is obviously far more cost-effective than expensive banner-based marketing campaigns. However, banner advertising is proving to be useless unless the banners promote companies, products, and services with the correct strategic fit for e-commerce (see Advertising on the Internet later in this chapter).

MONITORING WEB SITE USAGE

The Internet provides a company with much more of a marketing tool than just a web shop front. The Internet can be used to analyse which market sector is actually visiting your pages and for how long. Your company can even identify which particular pages interest which specific visitors. Your company can identify exactly who is interested and, more specifically, precisely what they are interested in. From this information your company can build up a highly valuable mailing list of people who have shown interest in your products and services.

Access logs are stored as plain text files that can be down-loaded from your ISP (using FTP) and opened in any word processor. They are normally arranged by time and date. To see how many individuals have actually visited your site, you would need to count the different user addresses that appear in the access logs or use a visitor counter.

If you have just published your web site then put the visitor counter on a page that only you know about, but refer it to your web site's index.html page to record the visitors to your content page. This prevents the initial embarrassment of your counter reading "you are visitor number 1".

When you rent web space you should ask if any of these reporting options are available to your company. The ISP should be able to inform you as to who looked at your pages, when and for how long. You can then use this information to provide highly targeted material, maintaining custom and develop a "customer relationship". This is one of the Internet's key marketing strengths.

These follow-up facilities provided by the Internet should not be ignored, as they could prove to be your company's most valuable marketing tool. A company can compose mailing lists of potential customers that can be targeted with special offers, gifts, free information and merchandising, etc. Your company could also use customer feedback to refine products and services to add value and increase market share.

ANALYSING ACCESS LOGS

It is worth spending some time at the end of each week looking at your access logs. An "access_log" will provide you with the total number, file names, IP addresses, dates and times of day of visits to your site. The IP addresses provide the unique address of the visitor, but you may not be able to use this to e-mail them, since many addresses are assigned randomly and change each time the visitor connects to the Internet. One part of the address that is un-likely to change is the country of origin of each individual visitor. There are several utility programs on the Internet (e.g. www.yahoo.com) that will analyse your access logs and list the visitors by country.

Some web browsers store information on the previous site at which your visitors have looked, known as a "reference_log". If you use a CGI script (computer gateway interface — a program that enables the server computer to record the answers given by users as they complete a web-based form) to query the visitor, it is possible to find out where they visited before they arrived at your site. This is a useful tool to check if there is a common point for the majority of the visitors. Perhaps they all see your site on one particular search engine, in which case check your entries on the others. If they all visit another commercial site before yours, that site should be contacted and a link or advertising banner should be offered. Visitors should be encouraged to sign a "guest book". This could, for example, give them entry to a prize draw or something similar. There are several scripts available that let you create a guest book.

GETTING FEEDBACK FROM CUSTOMERS

A company's selling strategy should facilitate relationship build-ing through two-way interaction with its customers. This can be achieved through allowing customers to contribute to your site, through opinions, preferences or reviews. This can forge customer loyalty, build a more intimate and personalised customer rela-tionship and lead to repeat purchases. Amazon.com asks its read-ers to provide comments on the books it sells. This is an excellent example of using customer feedback because the company gains extra value from its customers. When a potential customer now looks at the book that was reviewed they may be more inclined to buy it.

This relationship works well on the Internet. An Internet-based company should endeavour to initiate and maintain one-to-one relationships, and use customer feedback and involvement to help promote their products and services.

Online customers know what they want and have the technology to access it. If you provide the products or services that are *really* in demand, then use that customer demand to create further demand (by allowing customers to work for you, e.g. writing testimonials). You can then begin to create a "customer community" of your own.

One of the simplest ways to create customer feedback is to enquire directly what the customer specifically wants from your company, product or service. This can be done through the use of web site surveys and forms. HTML makes it possible to include electronic forms, which can be completed by home page users. This feature is extremely valuable for the following reasons:

- It can create network externalities.

- Customer information can be added to the company's customer database.

- Specific questions can be used to gather specific customer data.

- Any product preferences can be analysed, evaluated and acted upon.

- It can be used for low-cost customer surveys.

Internet-based companies will need forms to allow its web site visitors to enter text or choose from lists. Each ISP will have a slightly different way of providing this function, so it is best to e-mail the ISP for a guide to creating forms on a web page. They will probably send you an example which uses a special program to interpret the text a visitor has entered to either select a page or to send an e-mail message. Forms are very useful for choosing from fixed options or to allow a user to enter their name and address, comments or catalogue requests.

Two issues need to be addressed in order to ensure that electronic forms will work. First, page developers should contact their ISP to enquire if the computer that stores the form's web page has CGI capability. If a web site is managed by a computer without CGI capability its users will get error messages when they try to complete a form. Also, users may not have the kind of communications software that allows them to fill in forms as they view them.

The solution for both of these issues is to include specific directions for users to transfer the form to their own computers using a FTP. After they transfer the form to their own computer, they can complete it by using their own computer's word processing program and then send it back to the company by e-mail. This solution also applies to guest book features, which invite users to add their names and addresses to the company's database. Alternatively, an "e-mail us" hyperlink can be included on the page. This link leads to an e-mail message screen so that users can type in any comments or requests for specific information (see Chapter 13, Internet Utilities: Automatic Reply Service).

CORPORATE IMAGE

Using the Internet to promote brand recognition and enhance a company's image through newsletters, value-added information services, or requests for customer feedback and suggestions should lead to improved sales. Also, an Internet address is fast becoming a signal to customers that a company is progressive and up-to-date. Increasingly, traditional advertisements include companies' Internet addresses.

On the Internet, image is everything. If your business is based at home, to compete equally with global enterprises as a sole trader you may have to consider whether or not a home address should be used as the centre of a web-based enterprise. Instead, a PO Box address could be used. Some private mailbox companies, such as MailBoxes Etc (www.mbe.com) also accept incoming faxes and arrange any specialist postal services required. The concept of a "virtual office" can be completed by using global "lifetime" phone numbers, which can be used as the company number but re-routed directly to your company regardless of where you are at the time.

A company can have an office registered in any major city in the world if it opens an account with companies such as JFAX (www.jfax.com). JFAX will accept incoming voice mail and faxes, then digitally encode them and forward them to an e-mail in-box. Some ISPs will soon allow users to pick up e-mail over the telephone. Customers will be given a number they can call from anywhere in the world. Technology will convert the text messages into electronic speech and read them back to the caller. The service will be free but users will have to pay for the calls. Your company will be able to collect both voicemails and faxes on the same number, or set up separate numbers for each.

If your company is aiming to attract customers from abroad, these facilities make good sense; customers can get in touch with you without having to pay international call rates. These facilities will give the potential netshopper the impression that they are dealing with a well-resourced, highly professional, multinational company.

E-MALLS

An increasingly popular way for users to browse on the web is to visit an Internet shopping mall (an *e-mall*). This is a form of *piggyback selling* because users may first visit the mall in order to view one particular shop and then be attracted to other shops and occasionally make impulse purchases.

The big advantage of this approach is that the responsibility for marketing goods is shared between the business and the shopping mall owners. Depending on the type of shopping mall a company chooses they may also receive assistance in the way they set up their site. For example, the mall may collect payments on the company's behalf.

Shopping malls are an excellent way into e-commerce for some smaller business, but there are, at present, very few hosted in Europe. However, the US is generally ahead of Europe in terms of e-commerce, and there are hundreds of e-malls there. To get an idea of how these e-malls work access www.shopnow.com. One of the best-known UK e-malls is at www.barclaysquare. co.uk. Set up by Barclays bank, this site has a framework branding around its "e-shops", each of which is part of BarclaySquare. It has 14 shops, at the time of writing, including Interflora and Sainsbury's (see Plate 11.1).

PLATE 11.1: BARCLAYSQUARE

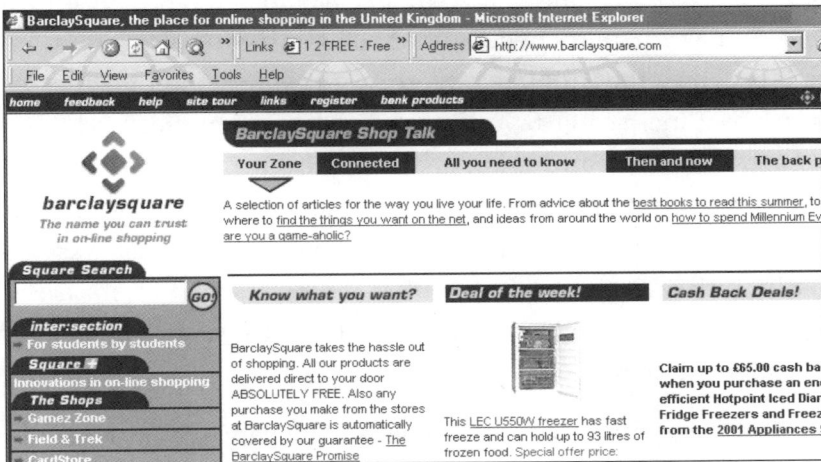

BarclaySquare also has a uniform payment method, which means customers can purchase from many shops before settling their account with one payment. The entry costs for a company joining an e-mall are relatively high in return for ease of administration and the security offered by Barclays. The popularity of this site has far exceeded its developers' expectations: during its first 10 months of operation, it logged almost 1.5 million requests to visit shops within the mall.

A similar service is provided by Enterprise City (www. enterprisecity.co.uk), Taxi (www.mytaxi.co.uk) and NetBenefit.[2] NetBenefit, the UK domain name registrar, has announced the launch of *I-Mall*, a cost-effective and efficient e-commerce solution for small businesses. I-Mall is designed to give businesses a shop window so that customers can browse products and services, make selections and place orders. It enables users to set up and review its catalogue from any computer and generate the store, shopping basket, and secure payment system, prior to uploading the details to NetBenefit's high-specification server.[3]

ADVERTISING ON THE INTERNET

The Net is building itself a niche as a complementary communication medium but, unless a company has the strategic fit for the Internet, many experts believe the web has a long way to go before it becomes the ultimate advertising tool for small businesses. It is finding increasing favour amongst large American advertisers, such as MasterCard and American Airlines, who have placed banner ads with big money US web sites, Excite and Netscape. In Europe, however, the reaction to online advertising has been decidedly muted; there is a feeling that there is not much return on any large initial investment for products and services outside the known Net audience:

> "The demographics of this medium are still very tight with the majority of users falling into the ABC1 category" (John Innes, electronic publisher at John Brown Publishing, 1998).[4]

The companies making most money from advertising on the Net are the search engine sites such as Alta Vista, Excite, or Yahoo! These sites, with the high volume of online traffic that passes through their pages daily, are the obvious place for a company to display its products or services to the Net-surfing public. Forrester Research predicts that Yahoo! will achieve £1,250 million in revenue by 2000. Yahoo! is confident that it offers the perfect medium to advertise online. Yahoo! sells advertising space on a per-impression basis (i.e. a company pays to have a certain number of pages that carry its banner advert).

In the US, Yahoo! is now selling a range of packages for advertisers based on "behaviour", not demographics, as search engines are beginning to realise that the narrow demographic sector online tend to display very similar behavioural characteristics and preferences.

New software is also available that deletes adverts from Internet pages and threatens to upset the Net's fragile economics. Software such as *Adfilter*, *InterMute*, *AtGuard* and Siemen's *Web Wash* enable computers to automatically filter out any type of advert. By removing adverts that consist of graphics, which take longer to download, these programs halve the time it takes to view a page and, consequently, the phone connection costs. Software of this kind will inevitably affect the future of the Internet advertising industry, where companies such as DoubleClick rely on providing thousands of web sites with millions of adverts from central databases.

> "This is a very fragile industry. This sort of software will not help it at all" (Mike Butcher, Editor of *New Media Age*, 1998).[5]

The only way to ensure profitability, regardless of the Net advertising format used, is not to rely on the technology of the Internet but to ensure those products and services you offer appeal to the profile of the known Internet audience.

In relative terms, getting a web presence is not expensive — the real cost comes in updating and maintaining a site. Businesses need to get away from the idea that having a web presence guarantees an automatic increase in sales. The Web is an anonymous environment and it is hard to quantify any customer response. Hit counters do not presently give any information as to whether or not a site visitor has bought anything.

So if your company is to make money from advertising online, the crucial question is, what form of advertising best suits your specific business to this specific medium? Certainly, as already explained, flexibility and precise audience target marketing are prerequisites of a successful Net campaign, but recent research shows that the traditional Net advertising banner format is not working. Consumers tend to be oblivious to the message a banner aims to convey or are annoyed by it:

> "Banners haven't been effective advertising tools to date as they fail to offer an invitation to action. The advertiser's problem is that they need to work out how to translate online ads into online traffic to their own web site. It's naïve to expect that it will work using the brand name banner as a paradigm. There's not enough substance to it" (Rob Norman, MD of CIA Media-network Interactive, 1998).[6]

Advertising must sell the Internet customer something that will either be of real help or appeal to them. This is known as *benefit selling* and is one of the most powerful forms of advertising. In TV adverts, the benefit is often implied: if you drink this particular brand, you will be more lively, happy, energetic and attractive to the opposite sex. In any medium the principle is the same: if your company offers a product or service that the potential customer believes they will benefit from, you are more likely to sell that product or service.

TARGET MARKETING

Most advertising and marketing experts recommend that Internet-related businesses should try to identify their target market and recognise their customer profile. By targeting customers you may achieve a respectable 5 per cent visitor/buyer ratio. Once you have attracted, and established, a sizeable customer base you should then attempt to retain customer loyalty through personal services and various loyalty-based schemes such as discounting for regular orders or direct debit payments.

The opportunity for competitive advantage is there for those businesses that support and interact with customers and build customer loyalty on an ongoing basis. By satisfying the requirements of relational marketing and transactions, companies may gain important insights into their customers' nature and needs. There is a need to establish these long-term customer relationships due to increasingly sophisticated customer demands.

One of the most efficient and user-friendly customer-data-capture programs is *Postcode Look Up*, developed by AFD (www.afd.co.uk), which automatically completes a data form when an Internet visitor types in a post code and house number.[7] Advances in information technology such as these have fundamentally altered the channels through which companies and customers maintain their relationships. The capacity to obtain and apply customer information within processes has become a key strategic issue. This often places the company in the position of requiring sensitive personal information from customers. This may create a new type of bond with customers. The importance of information exchange in relationship marketing, particularly using an electronic channel, requires a clear understanding and recognition of the potential problems (see Chapter 10, Attracting and Keeping Customers: Consumer Trust).

The Internet is a valuable tool for conducting and acquiring the following research on your target markets:

- Assessing the size of a potential market.

- Acquiring statistics relating to your target market.

- Investigating academic research on your target market.

- Evaluating competition and analysing competitors.

- Acquiring prices and pricing data.

In general, the Internet can be used to find out a considerable amount about any market sector. Regardless of whether a company invests in an Internet presence or not, it can still gain competitive advantage from the Internet by using it as a market research tool (see Chapter 14, Research on the Internet).

> "The pattern is clear. Today, Internet advertising is a niche market, used mainly by computer and Internet companies, and some segments that are suited to the wealthy male online audience" (William Reeve, Head of Fletcher Research's Internet practice, 1998).[8]

E-MAIL MARKETING

E-mail is the most prevalent Internet application currently in use. It is both fast and universally accessible, therefore it provides an excellent opportunity for direct, personal, target marketing (i.e. one-to-one marketing). To obtain customer e-mail addresses your company can do one or both of the following:

- Ask the customer directly for their e-mail address
- Track them through your web site access log.

Customers should then be asked if they would like to receive e-mail messages regarding your company's products etc. Most customers do not object to giving personal details, providing they know what happens with that information. Most customers also do not mind being e-mailed information about items they are genuinely interested in or derive value from.

Customer e-mail addresses can then be kept on a database. Customers can then be contacted individually, using e-mail and attachments, to make the customer aware of company news, newsletters, magazines, updates, upgrades and events etc. using HTML, graphics, video, audio and hyperlinks to carry a unique marketing message pertinent to each individual customer's requirements.

To use e-mail marketing effectively, a company should adhere to the following rules:

- Inform the customer what the e-mail refers to.

- Use the customers name or "personalise" it in some way.

- Allow the customer to refuse e-mails in the future.

- Include a fast "e-mail us" response link.

Before embarking on an e-mail marketing campaign, you should check that your ISP allows bulk e-mail in its "acceptable use" policies.

COMPETITION

Any company considering e-commerce should analyse and evaluate its competition. A company should investigate what its competitors do or offer and whether they already use the Internet to sell. If another company offers similar products or services it is important to offer those products or services cheaper or to "add value" to them. As much as possible should be investigated, analysed and evaluated about your competitors before committing to a marketing plan. To exclude any relevant information from the planning stage could result in an expensive misjudgement.

The Internet is a very fast moving and rapidly changing market environment. It is absolutely essential that your Internet marketing plans is as fully flexible as possible and avoids "strategic drift" away from your company's strategic objectives. A list of strategic options should help identify and evaluate contingency plans according to changing circumstances or customer demands.

THE MARKETING MIX

If your company simply adds the Internet to its existing marketing activities as part of "the mix" it provides, it will not exploit the potential of the Internet effectively. The Internet needs to be properly integrated within your company's ongoing marketing activities if it is to derive a significant benefit from it. For some companies, the Internet will be only a minor part of marketing, for others it will be central, and some companies may only exist because of the Internet. Most businesses will fall somewhere in between these two extremes.

The methods used to reach potential and established customers include: advertising, direct mail, public relations, posters, Internet pages, leaflets, point of sale material etc. Consider any innovative methods of marketing your business to complement your Internet marketing campaign. The Internet should be treated as a new opportunity rather than as a replacement for existing marketing and advertising. It may not be worth developing a web site at the expense of print advertising or mailshots. Both of these traditional marketing methods can be measured and will at least reach existing customers.

In conclusion, below are the advantages and disadvantages of marketing on the Internet, followed by a useful Checklist.

ADVANTAGES OF MARKETING ON THE INTERNET

- Global access to potential customers.

- Any enquiries or transactions are customer-led.

- Advertising costs can be inexpensive compared to traditional marketing methods.

- Customers can be tracked and identified individually.

- By adding value to products or services, through information or entertainment, a company can create long-term customer loyalty.

- The Internet provides the opportunity to make your marketing activities much more interesting and rewarding for the customer than previous marketing methods.

DISADVANTAGES OF MARKETING ON THE INTERNET

- There is currently a limited cross-section of potential customers.

- E-marketing is another separate element of your company's "marketing mix" that will consume time and resources.

- Direct competition is global and easily located by your customers.

- Advertising has to be regularly maintained and provide added-value.

- Most businesses cannot rely on the Internet alone for all their marketing.

Before your company can benefit from Internet marketing, it needs to evaluate how the Internet will enhance its current marketing activities, which of the advantages can be optimised and which of the disadvantages can be nullified. Constructing a marketing plan, or adapting an existing marketing plan, will enable your company to exploit Internet marketing more fully.

A marketing plan lists the ways in which a business intends to reach certain objectives. The sort of marketing operation devised will depend on the type of business proposed and the competition etc. At the initial stage, a business' primary objective is to attract first-time buyers, with a secondary aim of ensure that those customers repeat their orders. Therefore, the two-fold aim of a marketing plan is an extremely important one, as it has to create and maintain a buyer-seller relationship.

CHECKLIST

- Look at the Internet and decide on your approach.

- Decide on a host ISP that can support the front- and back-end structures you will require.

- Establish the business structure to cope with most eventualities.

- Announce the new web site to trade Journals.

- Register your web site with search engines.

- Submit your web site to computer magazine reviews.

- Include your web URL address in all company stationery.

- Create a signature for e-mail.

- Find relevant newsgroups.

- Spend time reading and participating in newsgroups.

- Look at alternative marketing schemes (such as banner swaps and link swaps).

- Keep your web site updated and reply to customer e-mail.

References

[1] www.nua.ie/surveys/how_many_online

[2] www.netbenefit.co.uk

[3] *Internet Works Magazine*, Summer 98, Issue 8, 1998, p. 20

[4] *Marketing Magazine,* 29 May, 1998, p. 27

[5] *Financial Mail on Sunday,* 11 October, 1998, p. 36

[6] *Campaign Magazine,* 22 May, 1998, p. 32

[7] www.afd.co.uk

[8] *Internet Works Magazine,* July, Issue 7, 1998, p. 10.

12

ELECTRONIC PAYMENTS

UNDERSTANDING THE INTERNET SALES ENVIRONMENT

The Internet audience is a sophisticated one and should not be underestimated. Customers who use your Internet shop will be making a special kind of purchase; they will not have seen or touched the product you provide and they will not have been able to test it. If you are selling a service, they will almost certainly never have spoken to you and will not have evaluated it. In other words, Internet purchases involve a considerable amount of consumer trust that is placed in you as a seller.

These factors play a significant part in determining which products and services have the correct strategic fit for Internet commerce. For example, viewing and advertising cars over the Net is becoming popular through sites such as Motor Trader (www.motortrader.com). However, few customers purchase cars without first test-driving them.

This is an important factor to realise, as your customers will expect higher levels of truthfulness and service than with most other methods of selling where they have been able to test products or examine any claims. Also, the demanding Internet customer expects their product or service immediately. These people are used to getting information quickly and expect a similar high-speed service for any purchases they make.

OFFERING INSTANT PAYMENT

Another important factor about selling methods on the Internet is that cash is almost non-existent. To conduct commerce over the Web your company will have to set up some form of customer payment procedure, such as a credit card payment facility. It is a fact that credit card holding customers spend 250 per cent more than any other customers online. Payment by credit card may be the most common and convenient payment method but it can be difficult and expensive to arrange.

Credit and debit card transactions are preferable because your customer may be thousands of miles away, in another time zone, using a different currency, and therefore you can not rely on cash. Cheque transactions slow down the proceedings, limit your cash flow and inhibit purchasers. Essentially, your Internet sales operation should try to allow people to make some kind of instant payment if you are to attract the maximum number of customers.

To conduct credit and debit card transactions from your web site, you will have to obtain credit facilities from your bank. The bank will probably insist that you use a secure server for any Internet commerce. Once a bank certifies your company for online commerce, you will be issued a Terminal ID (TID) and the bank will establish the TID with the company's credit card processor or service bureau. This is then communicated to the company when the company integrates the service into a new or existing web server application. A transactional server may have to be bought-in that encrypts credit card data.

ELECTRONIC PAYMENT METHODS

Payment methods on the Internet have raised a lot of discussion. Due particularly to the issue of consumer trust, some credit card companies have denied the use of credit card numbers on the Internet or, like American Express, have refused to conduct Internet transactions.[1] Consequently, major credit card companies and software sellers are building safeguards, such as a common Secure Electronic Transaction (SET) specification, for secure payments on the Net.[2]

In recent years some progress has been made in making the Net a safer place to do business. In the US, for instance, confidence in credit card-based transactions has flourished thanks to market acceptance of public-key encryption protocols such as Secure Sockets Layer (SSL) and, to a lesser extent, SET. SSL goes a long way to masking the data carried over the intrinsically public domain of the Internet, and does at least ensure, through its support of public-key certification, that any two parties to a transaction are who they say they are.

The impact of systems like SET could be significant because, according to Visa International, there has been no readily available secure way to prevent fraud or theft when giving out a Visa card number or other sensitive information over an open network. In April 1999, Visa International claimed that, even though Internet commerce accounts for only 1 per cent of all its transactions, 47 per cent of all transaction complaints and investigations were Internet-related.

For these reasons, Visa strongly encourages consumers, companies, and financial institutions to take precautions to minimise the risk of online fraud. Visa advises users to consider using online services only to browse for goods and services but to use the telephone, fax, or mail to complete the transaction, or if users decide to conduct transactions online to ensure that merchants are supporting security features such a SSL.

The majority of web browsers support this security system (including Netscape Navigator and Microsoft IE) as it is transparent to users. The downside is that it will cost you to set up a secure SSL site and you will have to pay a licence fee for the use of SSL.

If you are using an ISP to host your web site, check to see if they support a secure payment system. Many companies will not support a secure payment scheme until there is one that offers de-cent security outside the USA. Other ISPs have links to banks or provide SSL server security for all users.

IBM is expanding its Internet payment options, allowing consumers and companies to communicate even when they support different protocols. According to US reports, IBM plans to support a hybrid standard called *Moset*, which allows the two main technologies in this area, SSL and SET, to interoperate. The IBM scheme will enable consumers using SSL security, which is deployed in most web browsers, to pay for goods online with a credit card even if the company and bank involved use SET protocol.

There are various secure ways to pay on the Net, even without the SET or SSL specifications, from third party systems and certificate-based systems to Net money systems and smart cards.[3] SET may well be widely accepted as a paying method because, to compete, an electronic mall needs to support all common electronic paying methods and a method facilitated by large credit card companies may be the most common.

CHOOSING A PAYMENT SYSTEM

If you want to set up a shop on the Internet that allows customers to buy your products, then you will have to choose a secure system that allows your customers to pay securely. As mentioned previously, there are many ways of providing this security, but not all are ideal. While you wait for the technology to catch up, you could be losing sales so it is important to get a system up and working today. Credit card transactions are by far the most popular payment method, but even this method is still treated with suspicion by potential customers. Whatever method of payment you use you may choose to use individual customer accounts, giving customers unique IDs rather than having to transmit their credit card details across the Internet. There are several other practical solutions that offer flexibility and ease of use to your customers. At present a net shopper can use the following online payment methods:

- Credit and debit cards over the Internet

- Credit and debit cards by fax

- Cheques or credit/debit card details by post

- Vouchers

- Smart cards

- Electronic cash

- Electronic wallets

- Instant money transfers

- Traditional bank funds transfer.

Each of these methods are suitable for different kinds of transactions.

Credit and Debit Cards

Accepting credit and debit cards over the Internet is the simplest and most straightforward way of collecting money over the Internet. Many potential customers may be put off doing this because of the potential for unscrupulous third parties to copy credit card details and use them fraudulently. This is a theoretical risk rather than a practical one. In fact, sending your credit card details in the post or on a fax is, statistically, more dangerous.

You can increase the level of security in financial transactions by using the "secure forms" method of payment. This is available in most browser applications and it considerably reduces the potential risk of losing confidential information. Using the secure method of accepting payment a company can significantly increase customer confidence. More consumers use secure credit card payment methods even if, as most online card transactions still are, the transaction is cleared manually.

There are the following ways to set up a credit card payment facility:

- Use a merchant account with a bank
- Use a merchant agreement with a merchant servicing company
- Use a US-based card processor.

A Merchant Account with a Bank. If you already have a merchant account and accept credit cards over the counter then any online credit card facilities will be easier to arrange and less expensive than a start-up online business. However, to accept online credit card transactions new business must be granted a "merchant ID" by a card-acquiring bank. Online merchant accounts usually prohibit "card not present" transaction and impose application-processing fees, annual fees, "floor limits" on all sales and a percentage of each sale made.

The comparatively slow take-up of e-commerce in Europe is partly blamed on European banks' lack of flexibility in allowing small and medium-sized enterprises to conduct credit card transactions online. Presently, only 5 per cent of those companies that apply to banks for online credit card facilities are successful.

A Merchant Agreement with a Merchant Servicing Company. There are a few commercial software companies that provide all-in-one e-commerce solutions for web site hosting. Companies such as Actinic (www.actinic.com) and Shop Creator (www. shopcreator.com) offer merchant services including online accounts through specialist e-commerce banks such as NetBanx and World Pay.

Use a US-based Card Processor. The cheapest alternative to online card processing is to use a US-based clearing service, such as Kagi (www.kagi.com). Companies such as these list your products on their own server, accepting payment as an agent on your behalf, and clear funds manually. However, there will be currency conversion charges. Most payments clear within two to three days. Accounts are applied for online and there are no set-up charges. As usual, there are transaction charges and commission on sales.

Credit Cards by Fax

Accepting credit cards by fax is a facility worth providing for the many people who are still reluctant to send their credit card details over the Internet. You company can, even though it is less secure, accept payment via fax. The customer orders the products or services they require over the Internet and then faxes their credit card details.

Accepting Payment by Post

Accepting payment by post should still be made available to customers because not to provide every possible payment method will limit a company's potential market. Some customers may prefer to order goods and services over the Internet and may expect confirmation of their order by e-mail.

Vouchers

Vouchers are a new form of currency on the Internet. Such vouchers are not dissimilar to the gift vouchers available in most High Street retail outlets. The main difference is that they are electronic and are transferable. Indeed, the rapid rise in the popularity of such vouchers has led Internet pundits to predict that they may eventually become the most common form of payment.

You can credit your customers with electronic vouchers to be spent on products and services specific to your particular company. Customers can then exchange those vouchers amongst themselves, across the Internet, providing them with the same flexibility as cash. To buy your vouchers customers can supply you with their credit card details or send a cheque, or even pay in vouchers that can be used elsewhere on the Net. By providing its own payment vouchers your company can dramatically increase the possibility of sales and help build customer loyalty.

Smart Cards

Smart cards will trigger significant opportunities for IT sellers for the next few years. They are regarded by many experts as the fastest and most efficient way to secure electronic commerce, Web, intranet, extranet and workgroup applications.

Smart cards are a pre-loaded cash application that allows card-holding customers to pay for goods and services in the same way as conventional credit or debit cards. A single, multi-functional smart card has a chip that can hold user data on credit and can even be used as a travel card.

From a security viewpoint, smart cards are increasingly re-placing paper-based security applications. This is due to their flexibility, functionality and alleged security. Fingerprint biomet-rics, pass phrases, user names, and all other personal ID informa-tion can now be contained on smart card ID cards. Smart cards are the obvious medium for digital certificates and signatures.

Currently, there are a few camps vying to be the operating system of choice. One is Sun Microsystems (partnered with Visa and others) with a Java *Virtual Machine* (JVM) on a card. Another is *Maosco* (Multi Application Operating System Consortium), an industry-wide consortium which includes Mondex, Mastercard, Fujitsu, AmEx and others. Also, In November 1998 Microsoft launched *Smart Card for Windows*, its own operating system for smart cards.

Electronic Cash

Electronic cash, such as *CyberCash*, is suitable for small anony-mous payments for products from automatic retailers. To com-plete a transaction using "e-cash" requires the company's server to send its customer a digital receipt. A transaction can be captured and posted to a company's account while a customer is still online, or later if the company cannot ship the purchased product immediately. The CyberCash system supports host and/or terminal-based capture depending on an individual's bank system.

At the customer end, all CyberCash transactions are automatically added to a *log* contained within their CyberCash "wallet". At the company's end, all transactions are added along with all system actions into a transaction log (a series of databases). Transactions can be searched for and displayed individually or grouped by card types (MasterCard, Visa, AmEx etc.). The transaction records in this database are kept encrypted and only made available under password control.

CyberCash is actively working with the credit card associations towards standardising security for Internet commerce, including SET. CyberCash transactions are protected by a powerful and sophisticated system of encryption, combining DES private-key and RSA public-key encryption technologies.[4] CyberCash's 1,024-bit RSA encryption capability is the most powerful encryption technology currently licensed by the US government for export.

DigiCash (www.digicash.com) is similar to CyberCash in that it allows the customer to pay for goods anonymously, just like with cash. The customer and the seller require special software. The customer is given a special digital signature that authenticates a sale and the seller can then prove the customer has paid for the goods.

Electronic Wallets

Electronic wallets, offered by companies such as CheckFree and CyberCash, are online accounts that are stored on the customer's computer. This technology has been bought by CompuServe to allow any customer of CompuServe to buy goods over the Internet. Electronic wallets have some notable advantages over other secure payment systems. First, the wallet stores online purchasing data in a secure place. Second, when users sign up for the service they fill in their personal and credit card data only once.

Features include:

- It has a browser pop-up screen that requires no downloading.

- It calculates a company's billing forms and gives the consumer data while shopping.

- It uses 128-bit Secure Sockets Layer encryption.

Instant Money Transfers and Traditional Bank Funds Transfers

These work as follows: first the buyer authorises the bank to send money to the seller using reference information provided by the seller. When the money arrives at the seller's account, the bank informs the seller electronically and the seller's computer system fulfils the prepaid order. The alternatives to these online payments are standard cheque and postal payments.

Europe's first commercial Internet-based international payment system was launched by the UK-based travel and currency-exchange company Thomas Cook. It allows businesses to pay overseas suppliers electronically. Payments may be made by foreign currency draft or telegraphic transfer without forms or phone calls. Thomas Cook guarantees to process a transaction and confirm the full cost by e-mail and fax within two hours.[5]

The problem with encryption systems such as SET is that they are slow; transactions may take up to 30 seconds. Other criticisms levelled against SET include the costs, which will be incurred by both the customer and the bank. It will cost banks an estimated £1 million (€1.5 million) to set up the infrastructure to process SET transactions and a further £3 million (€4.6 million) to £5 million (€7.7 million) to set up each customer account.

However, SET promises both to make it harder for criminals to use stolen credit cards over the Internet and to make it easier for consumers to verify the authenticity of the companies they are buying from. It has been said that the need for SET is diminishing with so few criminals on the Internet and with adequate security systems built into browsers. The security risks in sending credit card numbers over a secure connection are, at present, considered minimal. There are more risks involved if the credit card numbers are stored in the seller's databases. In a credit card transaction both parties learn to know each other and that is not always desirable.

HANDLING INTERNET ORDERS

When customers browse your Internet shop they should be provided with a simple and efficient way of ordering. For this purpose, most Internet businesses use a straightforward order form. Products can be automatically added to the order form using hot links. As a customer selects a product by clicking on its name or picture, its details are added to the order. A simple ordering system such as this should improve order efficiency and increase your sales. A more complicated system, perhaps whereby customers have to type in the details of a product themselves, may lose valuable orders as it is time-consuming and adds to customers' phone bills.

Any order form should include easy-to-use payment options and you should always ask for the customer's e-mail address to keep them up-to-date on the progress of the order and to build up a valuable database of customer details.

MONITORING SALES

Regular and frequent checks should be made to account for every order made. These orders should then be processed as quickly, efficiently, and as accurately as possible. The global environment of the Internet may mean that your company will have to consider 24-hour sales systems. In any event, no company can afford to neglect its Internet sales operation, as Internet customers will expect a swift response to their orders. For reasons of security and consumer trust, the delivery of real products could be made by shipping them via courier to the customer.

TAXATION

The Organisation for Economic Co-operation and Development (OECD) Turkey Conference and the recent OECD Conference in Ottawa resolved to tax Internet transactions. It stated that the taxation of e-commerce should be relatively simple, should facilitate voluntary compliance, should not artificially advantage or disadvantage e-commerce over comparable traditional commerce, and should not unnecessarily hinder the development of e-commerce.[6] The resolution states that e-commerce should be taxed in the same way as non-electronic transactions, and that consumers should not have to pay tax twice on the same transaction. The OECD believes nations should draw up their own tax policies and that indirect taxes be levied on the basis of where a product is consumed rather than where it is produced.

The guidelines that the OECD has developed are not binding, but do indicate the path that governments are likely to follow. They are:

- No new taxes should be levied on goods purchased over the Internet.

- Digitised products, such as software, should also escape new taxes.

- The OECD will consult with computer security companies on encryption matters.

- The OECD will work with consumer groups to ensure that authentication codes are set. This way buyers will know that the people they are buying from are authentic businesses.

However, The European Commission does want to impose VAT on goods bought via the Net from outside the EU. Private European consumers who buy products or services on the Web from companies outside the EU currently do not pay tax. But the EU's new policy paper on electronic business states that if e-commerce expands rapidly, "the absence of such taxation would lead to unfair competition for EU operators" because they do have to add VAT to their prices. So, at present, the purchasing of goods and services over the Internet attract the same taxes as any other medium of commerce.

VAT

If your company is not registered for VAT (Value Added Tax), or you sell directly to countries outside the EU, then you do not have to pay any VAT. However, if your company is registered for VAT you must apply the correct rate of sales tax to goods supplied from your country of origin and delivered anywhere in the EU. VAT is normally charged in the country of supply. Therefore, according to the "distance selling" rule, if your sales rise above the levels set by the EU country you supply to, you should register for VAT in that country. If you do not register for VAT you cannot recover any VAT that may be charged by your suppliers.

To comply with EU legislation, you should obtain your customer's EU registration number and keep proof of export; a certificate of postage is usually sufficient. If you sell to private individuals, you should charge VAT at your country's rate. That is why US companies currently have an advantage over EU companies in that they do not have to charge VAT, thus reducing their prices.

References

[1] *Sunday Times*, (Sounding Off), 5 July 1998. P. 11.

[2] Visa International: *SET Specification,* http://www.visa.com/cgi-bin/vee/nt/ ecomm/set/intro.html?2+0.

[3] *Internet Business Magazine*, Issue 18, July 1998, p. 24.

[4] www.rsa.com.

[5] *Financial Mail on Sunday*, 9 August 1998. p. 7.

[6] OECD: *Dismantling the Barriers to Global Electronic Commerce*. http://www.oecd. org /sti/it/ec/prod/dismantl.htm.

13

INTERNET UTILITIES

INTEGRATING INTERNET UTILITIES

Any small business with a web site has to consider integrating it into the rest of the business and making best use of all Internet utilities relevant to that company's specific business sector.

For example, if a web site is intended to boost direct sales then a company should consider a telesales desk and staff to cope with any increased demand its web site may generate (providing that it wants to expand). If, for example, the company is selling a software product on the Web, it may consider arranging for the production of a time-limited, or cut-down, version of each package for potential customers to download. It is important to make sure that the web site is supported in a way that makes it an integral part of the organisation rather than an afterthought.

A single Internet connection offers a company the opportunity to integrate its business through the following range of services:

- *Sales*: providing product information, order-taking and 24 hour payment facilities.

- *Market research*: immediate information from the world news organisations, news groups, low-cost customer-satisfaction surveys, and voluntary customer feedback.

- *E-mail*: internal high-speed electronic communication between sales personnel, administrators and production personnel, the distribution department and all in-house staff. Also, suppliers, manufacturers and distributors outside the company.

- *Electronic catalogues*: the ability to provide on-screen catalogues of entire product lines with real-time updates.

- *Promotions*: gifts, discounts or on-screen presentations to highlight products and attract business, with 24-hour-a-day access for potential customers.

- *Information services*: providing information which highlights a product's usefulness, and adds value to the web site.

- *Entertainment*: providing humour, quizzes, amusing or unusual graphics or links etc. can all add value to a company's web site.

Although sales, market research, and promotion are available through other media, Internet technology now allows a business to focus on the buyers' needs and convenience at no added cost. The sales services on the above list are the result of a computer's capacity to store vast amounts of information and transmit it on request.

The key element is to organise information so those potential customers can gain easy access to the product details they want. web-based companies should attempt to build into their promotions a sense that they have anticipated their customers' needs in order to serve them better, enhance their image, and create brand loyalty for their products. No other sales media empowers the customer to choose both *what* they see and hear about a product and also *when* they receive that information. Therefore, it is worth evaluating how you can make best use of your company's web presence.

FTP

A web site is only one aspect of a company's overall web presence. Sites are supplemented by other facilities, such as FTP (file transfer protocol) and e-mail. FTP is a way of transferring files between two computers linked via the Internet. It is normally used to download a file from a distant computer or to upload your web pages to your ISP's Internet server.

You do not need to configure an FTP program. All you need to enter is the address (the URL) of the computer from which you want to transfer files. For example, if you want to download the latest version of Microsoft's Internet Explorer (IE.5), you would enter "ftp.microsoft.com" as the destination address. You may need to enter a user name and password but most computers allow anonymous log-ons.

ELECTRONIC MAIL

Nearly all ISPs offer free e-mail accounts, and related software, when a company establishes a web site with them. Electronic mail (e-mail) can boost productivity, improve communications, and cut costs. One of its cost-effective features is that an e-mail program can send as many mail messages as you like for the cost of a local telephone call. E-mail is faster and more reliable than any postal service and you know exactly when your message was read. An e-mail program also allows you to add "attachments" to your mail message by attaching any file or group of files to the message. E-mail can be a useful way of distributing data, receiving supplier receipts or getting customer feedback.

Any Internet-based company should consider receiving its user feedback through e-mail so it can follow-up that feedback at a personal level. This facility will become an integral part of Internet commerce as online firms realise the importance of establishing buyer-seller relationships through one-to-one marketing.

Electronic mail is transferred around the Internet using a system called *store-and-forward*, sending a mail message from your mailbox to the recipient's mailbox.

Every registered e-mail user on the Internet has a unique address that is normally written in the form "martin@thesuitcase. com". The section to the right of the @ sign is the company's domain name "thesuitcase". The section to the left of the @ sign is the user's name in that company "martin" (unique identifier). To send a mail message to another user on the Internet, you will need their full e-mail address, which includes their unique identifier and the domain name. As described above, this would have an @ sign (pronounced "at") in the middle and appear as shown above.

It is important to note that there is no permanent link between a user and their in-tray on an ISP. Therefore, the recipient will not know that they have received a new message until they next connect to the Internet, unless their company has its own in-house Internet server connected to their company network. Your electronic mail messages will be stored in your account on your Internet server (that is located either at your ISP or in your company) until you log in and read the messages. Some e-mail programs will start up automatically and collect any new mail messages as soon as you dial into your ISP. With other programs you will have to connect to the Internet and then start your e-mail program.

There are two ways to use e-mail programs: online and offline (i.e. whether you are connected to the Internet as you are typing out a mail message or you typed the message beforehand). To save costs on a dial-up Internet connection, several messages can be typed using your e-mail software in its offline mode (not connected to the Internet) and then, once you have dialled into the Internet, sent all at once.

As mentioned previously, this facility can also be used for sending files by e-mail as an attachment. Almost all electronic mail packages allow you to attach a file, such as a spreadsheet, to an e-mail message. The e-mail package will then encode the file and send it as normal to the recipient. When they receive the message, their mail package will decode the file and indicate that there is a file attached to the message, which the recipient can open within the appropriate spreadsheet software.

MAILING LISTS

Any company can subscribe to mailing lists that will automatically send you new reports, magazines or updates by e-mail. You can even use e-mail to send commands to other computers.

There are over 50,000 different mailing lists running on the Internet. They tend to be more specific in content than newsgroups. If you find a mailing list related to your company's interests, you can send a subscription message to the list server (a piece of software that manages the mailing list). Your subscription message has to include your e-mail address, which the list server will add to its internal mailing list. As soon as any member of the mailing list adds a message, it is automatically sent to every member on the mailing list. You can add messages or comment on existing messages and these too will be sent to the other members.

Provided you can find one relevant to your business, mailing lists are an efficient and cost-effective way of keeping up-to-date with your particular niche market. A directory of all the lists can be found at www.liszt.com.

Before you submit a new message to a mailing list, make sure that you have looked at the FAQ (frequently asked questions) document for the mailing list. This file or message will normally tell you the rules and conditions for new messages. For example, some mailing lists might not accept any advertising, others might not accept questions on how to use a product, etc.

AUTOMATIC REPLY SERVICE

One of the most useful applications of electronic mail is as an automatic response to sales enquiries sent by e-mail. For example, if you have set-up a direct "e-mail us" hyperlink on your web site for customers requesting information regarding a specific product or service, you may receive thousands of requests. Rather than having to reply to each message individually, you could set up an automatic reply system that sends a standard document about your range of products and services to any customer that sends a request. A customer sending mail for more "general information" would get a less specific e-mail back. Programs, such as Microsoft's *Exchange*, allow you to set up automatic reply systems.

INTERNET TELEPHONY

Being connected to the Internet provides a company with an alternative facility for making and receiving telephone calls. To set up a telephone system that uses the Internet you need to equip your computer with some extra hardware and run a special software program. You will need to add a sound card, speakers and a microphone to your computer (although some multimedia computers already have these fitted). The sound card converts sound from the microphone into a numeric form that can be handled by the computer and does the reverse when feeding sound to the speakers. Most web browsers now include the necessary requisites to support these telephone features. Otherwise you will need to buy an application such as Microsoft *NetMeeting*, *NetSpeak*, Intel *VideoPhone* or Netscape *Conference*.

Voice traffic over Internet Protocol-based networks (VoIP) includes both the Internet and private intranets. There are currently eight types of VoIP:

1. On-site IP Telephony. This allows for internal calls over IP-based LANs (Local Area Network).

2. Corporate Toll Bypass. Voice calls are made over internal IP networks or virtual private IP networks.

3. Voice Over the Net. Conducted between two multimedia-equipped PCs.

4. Fax Over the Net (mentioned in the next section).

5. IP-based Public Phone Service. Consolidation of voice and data over single IP core networks.

6. Call Centre IP Telephony. A separate application of voice/IP.

7. Voice Messaging over the Internet. Unified messaging over the Internet.

8. Video-over-IP.

Voice over the Net, direct PC-to-PC connection is by far the easiest to set up and use by plugging a telephone headset into a PC's sound card and using the appropriate software mentioned previously. It is then possible to use the Internet for telephone calls, providing that the people you are trying to call are also linked through the Internet.

All Internet activity is charged at local telephone call rates through your ISP. Therefore, in the near future the Internet may be able to use the telephone system to make and receive calls anywhere in the world at local call rates. For any company needing to make a lot of long distance or international calls, this Internet facility may be able to save them a substantial amount of money. However, the Internet's present poor real-time service means it is not yet suitable for most business calls.

INTERNET FAXING

In the same way that you can make telephone calls on the Internet, you can also send faxes. This saves money because every fax you send, as explained previously, is sent at local call rates (with a local ISP). Also, the recipient of any Internet faxing does not have to be an Internet user: faxes can be sent over the Internet to anyone who has a fax machine. However, there are some extra charges to pay, depending on which kind of Internet fax service you use. You will either need to buy specific software, or pay an Internet-based company to forward your fax on your behalf.

Whichever way you send a fax over the Internet it is always cheaper than sending faxes long distance, or internationally, using ordinary telephone lines. Experts estimate that small businesses can save up to 30 per cent of their call charges and larger businesses can save up to 50 per cent by faxing over the Internet. You can enquire about faxing over the Internet at the following web sites:

- http://faxsav.com/faxsavinternet

- http://www.faxscape.com

- http://ntxc.com

- http://www.netcentric.com.

Internal Communications

The Internet has led to a significant increase in the speed of business communications. Internal communications within an organisation can also be enhanced, and secured, with the use of an *intranet*. An intranet is a small, private internet with connections to the global Internet. An intranet exists only on a company's computer network and cannot be accessed by outsiders. An intranet uses web browsers in the same way, sending electronic mail, or perhaps taking part in video conferences, all using the same technology. The only difference is that your intranet can be restricted exclusively to your company. An intranet has the following advantages:

- It is secure.

- It is quicker to access (due to fewer users).

- It can still be used to access the full Internet using hot links (widening the scope of your company's own system).

If your business is large enough to require an internal communications system, it is well worth considering an intranet. It can improve business communication for many firms and provides companies with excellent methods of updating staff. Establishing an intranet is a highly logical step for many businesses, particularly those with more than one site. However, if you do decide to set-up an intranet, you may need specific hardware and software. You may also need one member of staff to be the Intranet administrator to work full time on running the system (see Chapter 8, Access to the Internet: Network Installation).

INTERNET SUPPLIERS

If it is a product, rather than a service, you intend to sell over the Internet, and you do not make that product yourself, you will require a trustworthy supplier. Once you have established a suitable supplier-buyer relationship for the products you intend selling, you should be able to place your orders online. Most Internet suppliers will provide an on-line order form for this purpose. You simply enter the details of your purchases, provide payment, give delivery instructions and then await your goods.

You may need to open an account with a supplier, providing credit card details, etc. In return for which you will be given an account number, which you can then use for any Internet transactions with that supplier. From a security point of view, because all activities on the Internet are traceable, it will be obvious if some other party attempts to use your account number. You should acquire a credit card that is used exclusively for business or company purchases. All of the leading credit card companies provide such commercial cards.

It is worthwhile remembering that even though some suppliers may look relatively inexpensive, this may not be the case. In some parts of the world where sales taxes apply, such as Value Added Tax (VAT) in Europe, businesses can benefit by reclaiming the tax portion of the costs. This provides a double benefit: the reclaimed tax makes purchases cheaper and the additional money can be invested before any portion needs repaying to the national tax authorities. However, many Internet suppliers fall outside such arrangements because they are acquiring their supplies from another country. Consequently, they may charge you a sales tax, which you may not be able to reclaim being outside their legal boundary. Equally, they may not charge VAT, reducing your ability to benefit from the VAT system in Europe.

Any receipts should be checked carefully. If your suppliers do not give receipts, you should send them an e-mail message with your suggested receipt details on it. You should ask them to respond with a message saying "agreed". Your e-mail pro forma receipt should then be re-quoted in their message. When you then print this out you will have an appropriate receipt for your accounts (see below, E-mail Receipts).

The following will help to get the most out of Internet purchasing:

- Ensure only one person (or department) is responsible for all purchases over the Internet.

- Have a credit card account that is used exclusively for Internet purchases.

- Make the most of intranets with an internal supply ordering system that goes through one central department.

Each company will require a different combination of these and other policies. However, you should have some kind of written company policy about what and when your company can order over the Internet, and how it should be done, otherwise you may encounter future problems and, possibly, lose money.

DIGITAL CASH VOUCHERS

Alternatively, you can open up a company digital cash account, whereby a company exchanges digital "vouchers" for the goods and services it purchases over the Internet. This is an increasingly popular way of performing business-to-business Internet transactions. The company providing the goods should allow you to purchase the digital cash vouchers according to your needs. Essentially, digital cash is the same as opening up a standard credit account with a supplier (i.e. as you buy goods or services, your available credit reduces).

E-MAIL RECEIPTS

Although most suppliers on the Internet provide delivery notes and receipts with any orders, some send an e-mail message as an itemised receipt. This receipt should be printed and processed through your accounts in the normal way, so that you can claim tax back on certain supplies.

VIDEO CONFERENCING

Video conferencing is still limited to niche applications due mainly to the lack of digital lines. The limited use of digital lines has mainly been due to their high cost. Now the appropriate equipment can be bought for under £1,000 (€1,550) and the technology may become more popular with European small businesses. However, most small businesses in Europe are restricted to using a single 128Kbps line, which allows for an unacceptably low refresh rate of the video picture. Therefore, until European telecos provide higher bandwidth communications options, video-conferencing will be limited to internal communications.

Those companies that may benefit from using video conferencing for business applications are those looking for potential increases in productivity and savings in travel costs. Creative meetings between designers or high-level meetings between senior managers also seem to be some of the better uses for this technology, though video-conferencing systems are less efficient on a one-to-one basis. Unless your business can make full use of this utility it is presently unlikely to be a cost-effective investment.

14

RESEARCH ON THE INTERNET

The highest percentage of Internet use is for research (information acquisition). The Internet has an almost infinite amount of freely available and instantly accessible information. Information that is now easily acquired was only recently often very hard to obtain in pre-Internet days.

One of the most relevant uses of Internet-related research for Internet companies is competitor analysis. By analysing any business competitors, your company will be able to decide its market placement by evaluating how your competitors are pitching their sales (i.e. in which market and to which geographical or demographic target). This research and analysis will help you determine your market placement and how to promote your business, i.e. through a unique selling point, niche marketing, competitive pricing, special offers or value-added services.

Internet-related research can also help acquire the following:

- Specific financial or management advice through the use of private, public and government sites (see Appendix 7).

- Potential markets through newsgroups etc. (see below, Using Newsgroups for Research).

- Potential business partners for networking or offering complimentary products or services to share links or banner swaps (see Chapter 11, Advertising and Marketing on the Internet: Links to Related Sites & Swap Banner Advertising).

- Cheapest components, goods, services, stationery etc. (see Chapter 4, Business-to-Business Internet Commerce).

- Overall trends in site design, value-added features, latest trends, latest consumer demands, state-of-the-art technologies, paradigm shifts, or any other features that could be incorporated into your site.

- Freeware or shareware. Invaluable software, such as WinZip (www.winzip.com), and design information, such as thumbnail programs (www.tucows.com) and meta tag advice (www.searchenginewatch.com), are all freely available on the Internet, provided you are prepared to search for it.

  Most software companies produce limited-use, or 30-day trials, of their products. Many of these products are downloadable directly from their company web site. For example, Macromedia (www. macromedia.com) provides free, 30-day trial, full versions of their web site development software such as FrontPage 2000, Dreamweaver.2, Fireworks.2 or Flash.4.

- Statistics and surveys. Many companies, such as Stat Market (www.statmarket.com), now provide regularly updated statistics and surveys, some of which can be e-mailed to you directly with any relevant information you have requested. Useful data may include statistics related to specific markets, most used technologies, most popular sites, etc.

HOW TO DO RESEARCH ON THE INTERNET

The Web presents information in a graphical and textual format, from which you can use your computer mouse to click on key words, pictures, logos, etc. These special "hypertext" facilities are called "hot" because from the homepage of any company's web site many other sites can be accessed through clicking on "hot" characters etc. such as "hot text". This dynamic nature of the Web is its key application.

Market research on the Web is made easy by a number of systems that use the hypertext utility, known as "search engines". Search engines are highly sophisticated hypertext-based computer programs that collect and index information from many sites and allow you to search the entire World Wide Web for information that matches any subject. According to Stat Market,[1] the following are currently the most popular search engines:

- Yahoo! (www.yahoo.com) The biggest and most popular search engine.

- Excite (www.excite.com)

- AltaVista (www.altavista.com)

- Infoseek (www.infoseek.com)

- MSN (www.msn.com)

- Web Crawler (www.webcrawler.com)

- Lycos (www.lycos.com)

- Hot Bot (www.hotbot.com)

- Snap (www.snap.com)

- Goto (www.goto.com).

Each of these search engines maintains a database of whatever content is available on the Web. These databases are kept up-to-date by access providers, companies, and individuals who publish their own material on the Web, and by the search companies themselves. When the search engine is activated, the database is scanned to find pages that contain material matching any key words. Because each search engine's database is different, it is worthwhile using two or more at any one time to retrieve all relevant available information.

An alternative is to use a search engine of search engines, such as Copernic 98 (www.copernic.com) or MetaCrawler (www. metacrawler.com). If you type a request into MetaCrawler the software searches the main search engines. It sorts results according to relevance and sends them back. Copernic 98, whose software has to be downloaded from the Internet, is even more sophisticated. Other engines include Excite! and Amazon's *ShopTheWeb* have branched out to offer shopping search robots.

RETRIEVING WEB PAGES

Whether you use hot links or type in the web address, you should be able to retrieve any relevant material to help in your market research. Any acquired information or data can be printed out as they appear or saved for later reading. The multimedia features used in web pages can be removed leaving only text. This will save phone costs and will make any web search faster and more efficient. Also, retrieving more than one page at a time can save considerable amounts of time and dramatically reduce your Internet-related costs. It is worth noting that in the EU, Internet data moves 20 per cent slower during weekdays after 7.00 pm CET and at weekends. This is due to the charge reduction in local call rates and the consequent increase in user numbers.

INTERNET ADDRESSES

All pages on the Web, similar to e-mail, have a unique address e.g. http://www.bbc.co.uk. "http:" stands for "Hyper Text Trans-fer Protocol". HyperText is the name given to the items in web pages that provide the hot links from one page to another. By clicking on a piece of hypertext the computers are instructed what to do. It is a highly sophisticated method of "turning over" a page, or closing one document and opening another. The two forward-slashes (//) separate the address from a piece of code telling the computer what kind of protocol to use for transferring the data, and "www" shows the user that the site is on the World Wide Web. The name in the middle of the URL is the company name (bbc.). A sign such as "co." refers to a registered company and ".uk" indicates it is based in the UK.

The Web is "case-sensitive" so any addresses should be copied exactly, including the correct use of capitals and lower case letters. Otherwise, if a character is misplaced or incorrect, the Internet search system will not be able to locate the correct web page.

INTERNET BROWSERS

Browsers are the software programs on which the search engines rely. They were developed to conduct data searches over the Internet. It is a browser's purpose to search through files taken from different databases to find the information which users request. Browsers enable users to visit sites, transmit content, and save files. They are designed to make Internet access easy and efficient, and help to locate sites when users do not know a specific URL address.

Browsers are stored either in the user's computer or with their ISP. They begin to work after an Internet connection is made. The user activates the browser by typing an address, clicking a mouse, or striking a key. All ISPs provide a space for the user's name, address or subject heading. ISP helplines, introductory Internet guides, and Internet magazines offer detailed advice on using browsers effectively. It is beneficial for Internet-based businesses to understand this process because it is what their potential customers have to carry out in order to visit their sites. The following are the four most popular Internet browsers:

- *Internet Explorer* (IE) is Microsoft's browser. It recently overtook Netscape as the world's most popular browser (see Appendix 1b).

- *Lynx* is a text-only browser, with no graphics; any non-text features included in a file will show up on the user's screen as blank space. Many older computers have low levels of memory and power, and are limited to using text-only browsers. web page developers may consider this when designing their home pages.

- *Mosaic* was the first browser with the ability to transmit colour and graphics, opening the way for colourful, dynamic web page presentations.

- *Navigator*, like Internet Explorer, is Netscape's advanced browser. Not only does this browser transmit colour, graphics and sound, but users can read text and move around the page while pictures and other features are still being copied by the browser, making visiting home pages less time-consuming.

Each search engine operates independently and has its own process for companies to apply for entry to its lists, but they all have in common the need for page developers to choose *key words* and phrases which describe the subjects that their home pages address. These words categorise the page and determine in which sections of the search engine's index it is to be listed. This may seem easy but it actually requires understanding how site visitors are likely to describe a product or service when they initiate their search. The most active search engines have *robots* ("bots") or *spiders* (automatic programs), which trawl throughout the Web reading home-page titles and section headings so that they can add any new items they find to their index. This means that references to home pages may be included in an index without any effort made by their developers if the pages have been designed with indexing in mind.

Search engines are only as good as the information they are given and are excessively pedantic about the correct spelling of keywords and phrases. The subjects being searched for should be typed within double quotation marks (" "). For more specific searches, a little logic and a tactical approach work best, plus use of the search engine's guidance pages, usually marked FAQ (frequently asked questions).

You should also use + and − symbols to further define your search. Typing a + in front of a keyword or phrase implies that it "must" be present in the matches found. Typing a − in front of a keyword or phrase implies that it definitely "must not" be present in any match. Your search should be as specific as possible, identifying what is unique about what you are searching for.

If your search produces hundreds of results, save the data to read offline when you are not connected to the Internet to save on your telephone bill. Do this using the File/Save As option in your web browser to save the data as a file on your hard disk. Alternatively, create a "bookmark" to this page within your browser and you can immediately get back to the page of results at any time.

USING NEWSGROUPS FOR RESEARCH

To get an idea of what is happening in a particular area of business or education, or to judge feedback on a particular idea or new product, you could look at user groups (often called newsgroups). Newsgroups make up an enormous section of the Net and they are getting bigger every day. Each section of the *newsnet* represents a specialist area and news groups can be found for most subjects. You should devise a marketing campaign that entails sending messages to the newsgroups that represent your target market. The message can then be read by anyone who logs on to that particular newsgroup. You can access these newsgroups either by using your web browser (if it can support this feature, i.e. Netscape Navigator) or by using a separate program.

To see the range of newsgroups available (there are more each day) you should enter the name of the server that manages the newsgroup feature at your ISP. Once you are connected, you will see a list of the available newsgroups. To see the messages in any newsgroup, double-click on its name and you will be able to view all the individual messages.

Messages in a newsgroup are organised in a hierarchical structure with original messages and responses to the original filed beneath it. This makes it easy to follow a particular discussion without getting lost. You can post your own message, asking if anyone knows about a subject or item that you might be researching.

USING E-MAIL FOR RESEARCH

You can use an "e-mail us" link to carry out e-mail market research on your customer. Any existing customers should be e-mailed about any special offers, etc. Using the reports from your ISP you can also e-mail potential customers, or those people who have visited your sales pages, but as yet have not bought anything. Your company may also be able to find other sites promoting complimentary goods and services and e-mail them to link to yours in exchange for a free link back. In this way people visiting other relevant sites will become aware of your company's site.

USING MAILING LISTS FOR RESEARCH

Mailing lists, or list servers, are rather like an automated mailshot you might send out to your customers to keep them up-to-date. In this case, a company has a mailing list to which you can subscribe. It will then automatically send, via e-mail messages, any news of new products or events that are of interest. To subscribe to a mailing list, you normally have to send a specific line of text to the mailing list computer via an e-mail message.

NEWS SERVICES

Most online news services are US-based, but do provide some UK and European news. If you want to keep up-to-date with news and reports you could take a look at the following sites:

- CNN (www.cnn.com) provides real-time news reports, analysis, weather and more.

- ABC (www.abc.com) provides a rival service to CNN with more emphasis on features.

- The BBC (www.bbc.co.uk) provides links to BBC programmes and news.

NEWSPAPERS

Most of the major newspapers are available in some form on the Internet. Some provide the complete text of the newspaper online, others include news and features. The following are some English language news sites:

- www.start4all.com. lists all the world's newspapers sorted by country.

- *The Daily Telegraph* (www.telegraph.co.uk) provides its complete text and back issues.

- *The Times* (www.the-times.co.uk) provides the complete text and back issues together with special features.

- *The Irish Times* (www.irish-times.ie) provides news from Ireland.

- *The Guardian* (www.guardian.co.uk) provides a cut-down version of its text.

- *The Evening Standard* (www.standard.co.uk) provides its full text.

- *The Financial Times* (www.ft.com) provides financial news and share prices.

- *The Wall Street Journal* (www.wsj.com) provides news with a financial emphasis.

- *Reuters* (www.reuters.com) provides world news as it breaks.

- *The Press Association* (www.pa.press.net) provides an hourly update of news headlines from around the world.

MAGAZINES

Many magazine publishers have placed their present and back issues online, and allow visitors to search for features and reviews. These provide a good source of background material and press clippings of product reviews etc. The best way to find a specific magazine is to use search engines such as Yahoo! or AltaVista for the magazine title, which will provide the publisher's name and the web site. Some magazines, like the recently re-vamped *Internet Business Magazine's* web site (www.ibmag.co.uk) are excellent research sources for most Internet-related businesses.

References

---

[1] www.statmarket.com

15

INTERNET SECURITY

Breaches of Internet security could treble by the year 2000, according to the US Computer Emergency Response Team (CERT). CERT has responded to more than 14,000 security incidents that have affected over 200,000 sites in the government and private sector. As a consequence, approximately 20 per cent of IT managers still view Internet security and consumer trust as the most important issue facing the IT industry.[1]

Other surveys reveal that 60 per cent of online consumers are concerned about Internet security issues. NOP Research Group's (www.nop.co.uk) recent Internet user survey shows that fear over security is still the main reason holding back online shopping.[2] Until these issues are addressed customers and business communities will not feel secure doing business online. Only when security and trust exist will e-commerce be allowed to fulfil its potential.

Companies expecting to conduct banking and other financial transactions over the Net should focus on confidentiality and data integrity so that customers and businesses alike can be assured that any data relating to them remains private and unmodified during transmission. There are obviously risks for small businesses in the Internet environment. The risks are mainly in the areas of electronic payments, marketing to the wrong audience, unsuccessful consumer trust creation, and insufficient site protection against hacking.

Electronic commerce and electronic business transactions handling are expected to decrease the obstacles of small business internationalisation and facilitate new business opportunities for small business. As outlined previously, practically anyone can build a web site to promote goods and services and begin business transactions via e-mail for comparatively low costs. All an entrepreneur needs is a computer, modem, adequate software and an Internet connection.

But regardless of the simplicity of e-commerce, until businesses and customers perceive it as an environment in which it is no more dangerous to conduct financial transactions than traditional marketplaces, e-commerce will continue to be viewed with suspicion. Because it is so easy to do business online and inexpensive to build an electronic point of sales, perhaps there is more reason to suspect that there is a high percentage of fraudulent and dishonest operators on the Net.

The International Chamber of Commerce (ICC), the world's largest private business group, is setting up a special unit to help companies around the globe combat cyber-crime. The new unit will work with Interpol, the international police organisation in charge of fighting crime across country borders. It will be an arm of the Paris-based ICC's Commercial Crime Services Unit and will work on crimes expected to boom in the Internet age such as money laundering, electronic fraud, industrial espionage and pornography.

RISK ANALYSIS

Every business solution that relies on high-tech products, especially computers and networking, has its risks. If a net presence is essential to the company the solution should be secured, for example, by using un-interruptable power. There should also be enough computing power to serve all clients adequately and enough bandwidth in communications. The server software must be capable of serving the clients with easy-to-understand human computer interface reliably and free of bugs.

The risk that somebody may cause the vendor's service to stop, or go offline, is always there. There are cases where hostile intruders have hacked into a computer system and prevented the authorised users to use the system. If this is possible, the intruders might do other things to harm the business, not only denying the service but also, for example, insulting customers or sending garbage mail from the hacked computer.

One of the main worries of businesses is that someone will be able to hack into their computers and extract confidential data, such as a competitor obtaining vital details about a product prior to its launch. Any illegal access such as this may well lead to loss of competitive advantage and any research and development investment. With a company computer connected to the outside world via the Internet, the theoretical risk of such industrial espionage is greatly increased.

The risk of security problems mainly occurs when a computer is permanently connected to the Internet through a system linked via a leased line hosting a web site. Many larger businesses prefer this option as it avoids the need to involve ISPs, thus retaining corporate control.

Having computers connected to the Internet means that anyone, from anywhere in the world, could connect to that system and conceivably do damage to it. This open global access to a company's web site is, after all, the main reason for establishing an Internet presence.

PROTECTING A WEB SITE

The majority of the world's web sites are largely unprotected. This fact raises the fundamental issues of security and the risk of sabotage. The point of setting up a web site is to allow the world to log on and view copies of a company's files without anybody being able to change them. If a company has downloadable software on its site (e.g. software applications) somebody, perhaps a competitor, may be able to log onto the server and replace it with a slightly different version, perhaps one that contains a virus.

Saboteurs have been known to replace a company's home page graphic with another unflattering version, edit the HTML code of a site, or log onto the server and delete facets of it. Hacking is part of the culture of the Internet. Some people do it for fun, others for more malicious reasons. A few hackers cannot resist a challenge, while some are excited by high-tech vandalism.

Security is most important when a company receives sensitive information over the Web, such as a customer's credit card details. It is possible to set up a secure system whereby the web browser and server negotiate an encryption algorithm. That way, all data transmitted is turned into code, which is unreadable to anybody else. A company can tell if it has a secure connection by looking at the location (URL) field. If the URL begins with https:// (instead of http://), the document comes from a secure server.

The security of a document can be verified by examining the security icons found, for example, in the bottom-left corner of a Netscape Navigator window and the colour bar across the top of the content area. The icon consists of a door key on a blue background to show secure documents and a broken door key on a grey background to show insecure documents. The door key has two teeth for high-grade encryption, and one tooth for medium-grade. The colour bar across the top of the content area is blue for secure and grey for insecure. Other browsers (such as Microsoft IE.5) use similar icons, such as padlocks etc. to provide the consumer with guides as to the security of a web site.

Renting space on secure servers is more expensive than conventional web space. If a company needs the technology it may find it best to put the majority of its pages on a normal server and then only the pages that require security on a more expensive secure system. This is quite easy to do, as web sites can link seamlessly from one server to the next without a user being aware. However, no system is completely secure; any hacker who can forge an IP address may gain access to any system.

RISK REDUCTION

You can reduce the risks of people hacking into your system and obtaining confidential data, however. The following ways of doing this are:

1. Server isolation

2. Removing sensitive data

3. Passwords.

Server Isolation

Your *server* is the computer, or its software, used to provide your Internet site. If this is your own machine it is best to make sure that it is not connected to other machines in the company. In other words, make your Internet server a *stand alone*, single computer. If at any time you need to obtain data from your company network, use floppy disks or other portable storage methods like cartridges to transfer the data.

Having an Internet machine linked permanently to your main network increases the risk of hacking. With the computer isolated, main data is much more secure and cannot be accessed by outsiders. Only the data you allow on the Internet computer can be seen. This is referred to as putting a "firewall" around a system (see Protecting a Network later in this chapter).

If you use an ISP's computer system it effectively isolates your main computer(s). Your pages will contain the material you send to the ISP and nothing else can reach the outside world, thus securing your own systems.

Removing Sensitive Data

If you split your computer network you decrease the chances of breaches in security. However, some businesses cannot have their main networks isolated from their Internet server. For example, if a company provides real-time data (e.g. stock market prices), updating an Internet computer without linking it to a main network would be impossible to stay up-to-date and competitive. You should isolate all parts of your company's network not required for the Internet by removing data that you do not want the outside world to see.

If, for example, your network includes real-time stock prices as well as a word processor and a customer database, but you only want your customers to see the real-time stock prices, you should move the other programs to another system. Essentially this means splitting the network, without changing the way any staff use their computer.

Passwords

Most companies renting web space update their site via FTP, logging on with a username and password. The user names and passwords may also be permanently stored on the same machine, so the FTP server can recognise the user when they log on. Some FTP programs remember user names and passwords if requested. This may be convenient, but it represents an opportunity for a hacker. A hacker may find where the passwords are stored and then have unlimited access to the site.

The weakest link of a security system is often the password. Passwords, which should contain a mixture of letters and numbers, should be changed as often as is practical. Some of the letters should be uppercase and some lower, and they should also be random. Also, meta tags can be used in an HTML document to prove authorship and the date of creation of any documents you may send by FTP to your ISP.

A company's ISP should take active measures against hacking and implement a sensible security strategy. Normally, a system is hackable if there is a bug in the software, it is incorrectly configured or, as previously mentioned, the password system is weak. Companies may request from their ISP where passwords are stored and how well they are encrypted.

ISP *Demon*, for example, has three completely separate password servers. The password servers do all of their negotiation on their own private network, and only then are users granted access to their site. ISPs should also change the default passwords, which come with its equipment and its routers. A router is a junction to the Internet which decides which packets go where and sends them accordingly. Unless the router is protected a hacker can see all of the traffic which goes through it.

Most unauthorised access to systems is committed by company staff. If one of the system administrators leaves Demon, the passwords in more than 90 UNIX machines are changed. Other companies may not be so vigilant.

Choosing a Password

Using passwords still remains the most common way of trying to reduce risk, providing authorised personnel with access to company web pages. Any person who has permission to copy files and change the contents of any page, etc. should be given a unique user-name and password. As noted above, the most secure type of password is a combination of numbers and both upper and lower case letters.

There are basically two levels of passwords: internal passwords and external passwords.

Internal Passwords

With internal passwords a company can ensure that only authorised personnel can change any part of its Internet system. This means that only specific members of staff can change your web pages or adapt the system in any way. Your password system should be confidential and staff should memorise passwords and never write them down.

External Passwords

External passwords protect Internet pages from being viewed by the unauthorised. Often, the homepage of a web site contains an application for a password to view or use other pages. Potential users of the system then apply for a password and may be notified via e-mail if their application has been successful and what their password is. Most companies provide passwords on payment of a fee. This enhances the service, and revenue, by enabling customers to view pages with greater detail than the more general pages provided.

Such a system of external passwords means you can control who uses your Internet pages. This system allows you to identify exactly who the users are, where they are from, what they are interested in, and their e-mail address.

MANAGING ACCESS TO A WEB SITE

Once you have set up your web site you might want to prevent users from accessing certain pages until they have applied for authorisation. For example, you might want to put up sales data for your sales representatives which you do not want anyone else to see. You might also want to publish a journal or newsletter on the Web, which you want to prevent users reading until they pay for the privilege. Lastly, you might want to monitor closely the type of customer who reads your pages, and in this instance you would want to set up a security system that asks the user to complete a registration form before being allowed to access the web site.

All of these scenarios make use of a password authorisation feature that is available with most ISPs and with an internal company Internet server. It works as follows: you place the web pages that you want to protect into a special directory on the web server. In this directory you create a user-password file. Each time a user tries to access a web page that is stored in this directory, the web server software will pop-up a dialog box asking the user to enter a user-name and password. The software then checks this against the file and allows access if there is a correct match.

To set up this type of security is straightforward but it will vary depending on the type of web server software you or your ISP are using. One way of creating a protected site would be to follow these steps:

- Create a home page asking the user if they have registered with your company.

- If the user has not registered, display the web page with a registration form.

- This form is submitted to an authentication program that generates a unique user-name and password for this user. These are also automatically stored in the user-password file.

- If a user has registered, then they can view the web pages in the protected directory.

- The action of calling up a page in the protected directory will automatically prompt the user to enter their name and password. If these are correct, the page may be viewed.

SECURITY MEASURES

Web browsers include a degree of security devices, which mean that any company system is more highly protected than before. However, these "secure" transactions on the Internet can still be breached. Indeed, there are hackers who earn a living by keeping one step ahead of the security measures in the current range of browsers. Even though they are significant and can provide you with considerable help, companies who consider their web site content a potential target for hacking should not rely on browser security measures alone.

Your Internet machine may be secure but it could be damaged through a malicious piece of computer code called a "computer virus". These software programs are attached to other, innocuous, pieces of code, such as free programs downloaded from the Net or data from an imported file or e-mail. Once the virus is resident in a computer it can cause havoc, potentially deleting all of a company's data. It may also reproduce itself, attaching itself to files making them unusable, or just display harmless but annoying messages. Mainly emanating from Eastern Europe and America, there now exists a virus industry for which the Internet provides a highly suitable method of transferring viruses from one computer to another.

Avoiding Virus Infections

To avoid infection the following precautions should be taken:

- Use anti-virus programs on all computers.

- Use anti-virus programs for all Internet usage.

- Conduct regular computer "health checks".

Every business-related computer in a company should have anti-virus protection. There are many excellent and inexpensive programs available. Not using anti-virus programs to protect all Internet connected computers exposes your company to a significant potential risk.

Internet anti-virus software can detect incoming viruses and warn you before they reach your computer. If the virus does get to your computer from the Internet, these programs can eliminate them before they do any damage. Anti-virus programs are an almost vital requirement for any businesses conducting Internet commerce. The use of *applets* (small programs to create web page features and facilities) has increased the opportunities for hackers to use the Internet for malicious intent. Regular "health checks" should include checking your computers for hard disk problems and viruses as well as the detection of malignant applets.

INTEGRITY

Risks related to data and data transfer can be avoided by using common sense and employing encryption methods or other security tools. Trading partners should also be made aware of the possibilities of data corruption and theft. In electronic business conversations, both parties must be certain that information arrives with precisely the same contents as it was sent. That means that nothing is added, taken away, or altered during the data transfer. The integrity of a message can be secured using digital signatures.

DIGITAL SIGNATURES

Digital signatures have a similar function to traditional hand written signatures, namely to identify the signatory in such a way that the recipient has legal irrefutable proof that the named individual approved a document, agreed to a transaction, or was present at a particular moment. As a crucial part of the foundation for commerce, law and social order, it is essential to retain these characteristics in developing security technologies, while it is also clear that the traditional signature may no longer be able to continue to perform its historical function in electronic commerce.

Digital signatures are based on a class of codes that have two keys. What is encrypted by one key can be decrypted only by the other and vice-versa. If someone keeps one key private while making the other public, then any text that can be decrypted with their public key could have been encrypted only with their private key, and therefore only by them. Such texts are "signed" by the user. In some ways, such signatures represent a higher degree of authenticity than written signatures because they are harder to forge, although they can be "stolen" electronically.

An especially attractive feature of digital signatures is their ability to allow a text to be signed by many people. For example, a text can be encrypted once by a procurement officer, then mailed to their superior who will encrypt it again with their private key, and finally mailed again to the bank holding the company's credit line for a third pass. A company decrypting such a purchase order can be confident of the identity of the person making the order, that they had the authority to make the order, and that the company has the credit to support the purchase.

Similarly, a digitally-signed response to a *request for payment* (RFP) might come signed with one key from a party certifying that the bidder had a good credit balance and another from a reference bureau, testifying to their work history. While all of these functions could certainly be performed on paper or with EDI, digital signatures are cheaper, faster and more flexible. As important as the security applications of the technology might be, many feel its future will be as a management tool.

Digital signatures provide two things: assurance that the message is from the purported sender, and that the message has not been altered since it was signed.

ENDORSE[3] is a UK government-backed initiative to use electronic coding to provide a digital signature via a smart card, sent via the Internet to government, initially to be for the registration of self-employment. The UK government hopes that this method of commerce will be extended to applications such as tax self-assessment, etc.

For the moment, digital signatures exist in a benign legal limbo. Their usual application is in cheap browser-server authentication (as in SSL). Companies accept no liability whatever for these exchanges, but the technology is acceptable. Beyond this is a range of experiments within networks of established business relationships, often using intranets or extranets. These are controlled by negotiations worked out on a case-by-case basis, by pre-existing contractual relationships, or by regulations governing the overall business mission; such as the rules defining credit card liability.

Copyright and Confidential Data

To deliver copyrighted items through the Net and maintain the copyright is difficult. Even if the copyright stays with the copyright owner there is practically no way of controlling what the receiver does with the data. The legislation is already in place in most countries but there is not any party to control the situation. To transmit confidential data the simple solution is to use cryptography. Even though the US, and other governments, has been wise enough to forbid the export of some efficient encryption software products there are a variety of solutions available. Secret data, such as data that those not involved are unauthorised to review, should not be risked on transmissions through public networks.

Protecting a Network

If we are to believe the advertisements, a *firewall* is the cornerstone of network security. The first point to make is that there is no need to install a firewall unless you have a direct link between the Internet and your office network. For example, if you have installed an Internet server in your office and have connected it to your company network, then you need a firewall. If, however, you dial into the Internet on an occasional basis to check for electronic mail or to maintain a web site stored on an ISP's server, then you do not need a firewall.

A firewall is a security mechanism to prevent information leakage.[4] A firewall's purpose is to protect the entrance to a network and make sure nothing untoward gets in. It controls access based on identification of incoming visitors and then keeps records of these visits, or attempted visits. A firewall is easy enough to install, and most companies already recognise their importance, though firewalls cannot be used if a company is renting space on somebody else's server.

A firewall is little more than a computer equipped with two or more network adaptors. A piece of software determines which forms of network traffic are allowed between those adaptors. This software, in effect, functions as a wall with small holes in it that allow only certain items to pass through unrestricted. In most cases, powerful server hardware is required, together with a server licence, and firewall software. Some firewalls come with a one-off software charge, other providers may charge per simultaneous user.

Two types of firewall exist: the first is the so-called *filtering* firewall. This is the most basic type. It looks at the header of each TCP/IP packet that enters the system and determines if it will pass or be discarded. It does this based on the Internet protocol (IP) address found in the header and the port-number specific for various types of network traffic. The second type of firewall is the *application* or *proxy* firewall. In this type of firewall, no direct traffic between two or more networks is allowed. Instead, all communications are routed through specific applications running on the firewall called *proxy servers*. Most firewalls use a combination of both systems.

Today, firewalls are a lot more than just simple gatekeepers that guard the entrance to a network. The main reason for this is the growing use of the Internet, in particular the use of the Net as an extranet, an extension of a private wide area network (WAN) to facilitate remote access. The Internet is an open network where anybody can intercept information, therefore, all connections to the firewall and the network behind it need to be encrypted using a safe encryption algorithm creating a *virtual private network* (VPN). Extranets applications require additional security measures. Users have to identify themselves if they want access. Traditionally, this is done by entering a user name and password, but systems such as smart cards can be used.

A recent US study of 400 companies by the FBI discovered that a third of all successful external break-ins via the Internet happened despite the presence of a firewall and 90 per cent of web sites can be penetrated and shut down within 10 minutes:

> "It is usually only a matter of hours before the hacker can gain access to the entire IT system. Firewalls are often not put on the right place on the network or are not properly configured" (Harry Ram, Director of Communications for Diligence Ltd., 1998).[5]

The growing realisation is that firewalls can be deeply flawed and a more holistic approach to network defence needs to be taken. There are now two main schools of thought on how a firewall can be installed in a network. The first is that firewall software, usually using a common operating system, should be placed on a server, the proxy firewall. The second is that a separate box with its software, usually written in a proprietary language, should be placed between the Internet and the web server, the state inspection wall. The problem is that neither of the main two systems has been completely successful in stopping attacks.

> "However good the firewall and its configuration, it still has security policies based on IP addresses, which is a fundamentally flawed methodology" (Andy Kemshall, Principal Consultant for Security Dynamics, 1998).[6]

The differences in price and performance of firewalls are so enormous that care should be taken when considering your company's requirements. The right price includes hardware, software and support. Unfortunately, for the smallest of businesses it appears that, like so many facets of new technology, a high level of secure and efficient e-commerce is only available to those that can afford it. However, small businesses should be reassured that breaches of web site security are very rare and that 98 per cent of all security breaches are thought to be "inside jobs" committed by employees!

RELIABILITY

Ultimately, one of the most vital elements of Internet security and consumer trust is the reliability of the Web as a means by which e-commerce is conducted. Recently, due mainly to the increasing demands on its bandwidth, the Net has witnessed a number of significant "outages" (network failures) causing a loss of Internet access, etc.[7] Many organisations, towns, cities, and even small countries rely on a single length of fragile optical fibre for their connection to the main Internet backbone; this scenario is commonly known as "back-hauling". Due to this situation there are an increasing amount of net failures.

> "The bandwidth on the Net doubles every nine to twelve months but traffic is eating up the bandwidth" (Bob Metcalfe, Head of Research at IDG, 1998).[8]

Unless businesses and customers can be convinced there is a secure future for e-commerce, including network reliability, few potential customers will use it and fewer businesses will invest in it. Who can blame them when telecommunications experts are unsure of the Net's future reliability:

> "The telephone network was originally dimensioned for people who on average would make three or four four-minute phone calls a day. That gives a peak-to-mean ratio of around 4:1. But the Internet, which has simply been tagged on top of our existing 100-year-old phone network, makes the ratio nearer 1,000:1. Ergo, you need a different kind of network and a different approach to the technology to cope. If not, by 2003, when it's predicted that Internet traffic will overtake telephone traffic, the parasite might kill the host by swamping it" (Peter Cochrane, Head of Applied Research and Technology for BT, 1998).[9]

The increase in Internet usage in the UK, driven by subscription-free services, has doubled connection failure rates. On average, one in ten attempts to log on now fail. The take-up of free Internet access has been so big that all the ISPs have benefited but, similar to the US, the UK networks cannot cope sufficiently. As the rest of Europe move towards free Internet access, and the consequent increase in demand, its telephone line networks will also have to tolerate an ever-increasing work load.

References

[1] *Financial Mail on Sunday*, 16 August 1998. p. 10

[2] *Sunday Times*, (Innovation), 6 September 1998. p. 6

[3] *Business Lunch*, BBC2, 17 June 1998

[4] Tanenbaum, A. S., *Computer Networks* 3rd ed. (Prentice Hall International Ltd.: London) 1996, p. 410

[5] *Computing*, 8 October 1998, p. 4

[6] *Network News*, 30 September 1998, p. 18

[7] *Business Lunch*, BBC 2, 17 June 1998

[8] it@mailonsunday.co.uk

[9] *Computer Bulletin*, September 1998, p. 20.

16

CONCLUSIONS

The advantages of Internet commerce for any small business suited to e-commerce are the relatively inexpensive start-up costs, the huge potential customer base and the precise target marketing opportunities. How small businesses can make best use of the Internet is, most importantly, to create the correct *strategic fit* for Internet commerce.

If your product or service is suitable for net marketing and electronic commerce, the Internet provides a huge but heterogeneous marketplace. The current Internet audience has such a narrow demographic range that the products and services that appeal to this limited customer base is equally limited. Nua[1] estimates that only 2.4 per cent of the population worldwide (115.75 million people) are online, and currently only 14 per cent (2.5 million) of WWW users have purchased products or services over the Internet.

> "For every rising star of online commerce, there are huge dark spaces in between" (Heather Starck, Principal Consultant, Ovum Consultancy, 1998).[2]

Internet commerce is increasingly niche-driven. Those companies that have specialised in niche markets and have used the World Wide Web to achieve a wider market-share have already achieved competitive advantage over similar companies who have yet to trade on the Internet. Those companies providing products that require a great deal of information, or whose products or services are suited to browsing, such as book sales, record sales or ticket services, e.g. travel agencies and theatre tickets, have also achieved competitive advantage. Specialisation and browsing facilities seem to be common denominators of successful online businesses. This is an example of how the public are prepared to browse the Web if it results in cheaper prices, especially if the Internet gives customers access to the same information as any "middle man" or agency.

Sellers or producers of items either difficult to obtain in Europe or cheaper to buy outside Europe (after VAT and import tax), are also in profit, as are manufacturers of bespoke items. The Internet has also created new business opportunities for those who produce web site content or access to the Net.

Clearly, if a company can attract potential customers through accurate target marketing it may create a profitable customer base. By being the first to market, or perhaps creating demand for a new product or service, your company should also secure the largest market share and establish its brand online.

If you are considering going online, you should first evaluate whether or not your company has the correct strategic fit for e-commerce. Look at the Internet and decide your approach and define your target market. Target a specific customer profile that you know uses the Internet. Use all the Internet utilities to acquire as many statistics and research as possible relating to your intended target market and possible competition. As an Internet advertiser, you should target your efforts towards developing an interactive buyer-seller relationship based on inducements, added-value content and customer feedback.

Your online corporate image should be the equal of any large corporation. It is import to create a strong, well-defined brand name, whether it is based around your company's name, products or services, and registering it as a domain name as soon as is feasible. You should get your web site address listed with as many search engines and directory indexes as possible and promote your site through all available mediums, not just the Internet. Your biggest challenge will be to integrate your web site into your existing corporate structure, strategies and image your company may have already established.

Your web site should have user-friendly functionality and be appealing to your target customers. Visitors should only be two or three clicks away from what they are looking for. It should also have appropriate hyperlinks and legal content. As an online company you should be aware of future IT developments and the direction e-commerce is likely to take in the future. For example, small hand-held devices and integrated television, which will dominate the future of e-commerce, are not suited to scrolling but smaller, single frames and pages and navigation buttons.

You should try to provide all appropriate payment methods for your particular business and try to obtain credit card payment facilities. You should also consider carefully which delivery system you will require. Be honest with your customers: give accurate prices and realistic delivery times and try to support your products with a guarantee or issue a statement of customer service and offer customer support. Calculate all taxes and handling charges and include them in your web page. Try to provide a premium service: customer care, payment and delivery guarantees. Your goal should be to establish the business structure, including user-friendly ordering, secure payment and timely delivery systems, to cope with most eventualities.

You will want to attract and identify new customers while nurturing your best customers through your customer purchase history records to personalise dialogue with customers. By analysing your visitor logs you can monitor buyer behaviour and build a customer database. You should attempt to build a buyer-seller relationship and consumer trust by encouraging customer participation and personal information, i.e. find out what your customer wants from you.

Always try to create a customer community by making the customer feel comfortable and involved with your site. To keep up-to-date with online customer trends, you should use the Usenet news groups to help promote your web site. You should keep your web site updated and reply to all customer e-mail and reward your loyal customers with discounts, offers or gifts. Occasionally, you should evaluate those promotional activities that are affective and those that are not.

Depending on which industry you are in, you should also consider selling to other businesses. Business-to-business commerce is currently the most popular use of e-commerce, especially for those companies using EDI. Opportunities are expected to increase for small businesses to provide products or services complementary to other businesses through the Net. There would seem to be adequate opportunities for small producers of indirect goods and non-strategic products to trade directly with larger organisations through "spontaneous electronic commerce" such as EDI and EFTS. Opportunities such as these are expected to increase over the next few years as this sector of e-commerce is set to expand steadily.

The advent of digital television, and Internet facilities provided for all European schools, will increase both Internet access and familiarity. This will provide millions of potential Internet customers able to access the Web through the familiar mode that TV provides. This fact will inevitably impact on the future of electronic commerce over the Internet, increasing the opportunities for small businesses to make money, but also intensifying the necessity for competitive advantage through added-value services.

Even if a global television-based media does dominate all levels of marketing and commerce in the future, the Internet is guaranteed to become a mass media in its own right, whether it exists on portable, hand-held devices alongside TV or is integrated within it. The small business sector will be supported increasingly by future Internet-enhancing technologies. Therefore, if your company has the strategic fit for e-commerce, it should not hesitate in planning an Internet presence.

Although the larger Internet audience of the future will inevitably allow for a greater cross-section of businesses to trade successfully on the Internet, ultimately, strategic fit will remain *the* most vital consideration for any small business considering going online. Strategic fit (that is, whether the goods and services offered by a company match the currently narrow socio-demographic profile of current Internet consumers) is the most important determinant as to whether the smallest of businesses can achieve cost-effective competitive advantage.

Hopefully, following the advice within this book, as a small businesses owner-manager you should now be able to evaluate whether your business is likely to be successful in Internet commerce and if it is, how best to build, market and maintain your Internet presence.

References

[1] www.nua.com

[2] *Computing*, 6 November 1998, p. 20.

APPENDICES

APPENDIX 1

a) Demographic Profile of Net User

- Age: 22-30
- Male/Female: 69%/31%
- Married/Single: 40%/60%
- University educated: 50% (18% are educated to postgraduate level).
- Average income: $31,000 (£19,375 or €30,000)
- 30% are likely to have salaries in excess of £40,000
- 55% claiming to use it for work purposes
- 30% for pleasure and 15% for education
- 33% are in the banking/finance sector
- 23% in agriculture
- 15% in education
- 34% are in a managerial/administrative position
- 30% are professional
- 9% are skilled manual labour

- 66% use a Netscape browser

- 33% opt for Microsoft IE.

Source: *Redsquare* (1998)

b) More recent surveys suggest that Microsoft have now overtaken Netscape as the most used Internet browser:

Web Browsers	*% of users*
Microsoft	72.30%
Netscape	25.74%
Other	1.96%

Source: www.statmarket.com/sm?c=browsers. (June 1999)

The typical net user profile: 84.5% male   82.3% white[1]

---

[1] *The Net* BBC2, 2 February, 1998

APPENDIX 2: INTERNET POPULATION

a). Internet Population Projected Growth:

Date	Population (in millions)
1995	22
1996	37.84
1997	58
1998	87.75
1999	110.25
2000	132.75

b). World Wide Web Population Projected Growth:

Date	Population (In millions)
1995	14.3
1996	25.96
1997	48
1998	76.5
1999	101.25
2000	126

Source: Binary Compass Enterprises 1998

c). Actual Internet Population:

Canada & USA	88, 330, 000
Europe	37, 150, 000
Asia/Pacific	26, 970, 000

The current global population online is 159 million.

Source: www.nua.ie/surveys/how_many_online. June, 1999.

[Appendix 3a]

APPENDIX 3

a). Internet Service Providers (ISPs) in the UK:

Name	Free Trial	Set-up Fee	Monthly Charge	No. of E-mail Accounts	Free Web Space	Web site
BT Internet	No	N/A	£11.75	5	10 Mb	www.btinternet.com
Cable & Wireless Internet	No	£10.00	£10.00	5	5 Mb	www.cwcom.net
ClaraNet	One Month	N/A	£11.63	No limit	25 Mb	www.clara.net
Demon Internet	One Month	£14.49	£11.75	No limit	15 Mb	www.demon.net
Direct Connection	No	N/A	£13.50	No limit	20 Mb	www.dircon.net
EasyNet	One Month	N/A	£11.99	No limit	No limit	www.easynet.co.uk
Global Internet	One Month	N/A	£10.39	No limit	50 Mb	www.global.net.uk
Netcom	One Month	N/A	£14.95	10	10 Mb	www.netcom.net.uk
Pipex Dial	One Month	£13.51	£14.98	5	15 Mb	www.dial.pipex.com
Virgin	One Month	N/A	£11.99	5	10 Mb	www.virgin.net

Source: www.netcraft.com/survey/

[Appendix 3b]

APPENDIX 3 CONT'D

b). Free Internet Service providers:

Name	Set-up Fee	Support Line Costs	E-mail Accounts	Free Web Space	Web Site
BT Click Free	N/A	50p per min	No limit	N/A	www.btclickfree.com
Cable & Wireless Lite	£10.00	8p max per min	1	N/A	www.cwcom.net
Connect Free	N/A	50p per min	No limit	N/A	www.connectfree.co.uk
Free-Online	N/A	50p per min	No limit	No limit	www.free-online.net
Freeserve	N/A	50p per min	No limit	15 Mb	www.freeserve.co.uk
TescoNet	N/A	50p per min	5	10 Mb	www.tesco.co.uk
X-Stream	N/A	50p per min	1	20 Mb	www.x-stream.com

Source: IT Mail, 3 February, 1999.

[Appendix 3c]

c). Online Services:

Name	Free Trial	Monthly Charge	No. of E-mail Accounts	Free Web Space	Web Site
AOL	One Month	£16.95	5	10 Mb	www.uk.aol.com
CompuServe	One Month	£17.95	1	5 Mb	www.compuserve.com
LineOne	One Month	£9.99	5	10 Mb	www.lineone.net
MSN	One Month	£14.95	1	5 Mb	www.msn.com

None of the above service providers charge a set up fee.

Source: IT Mail, 3 February, 1999.

APPENDIX 4

US Consumers Average Online

Median Age	33.33
Male/Female	68% / 32%
Married/Single	41% / 59%
College educated	47%
Average Income	$31,000 (€29,300)

Source: Jupiter Communications

APPENDIX 5

a). Profile of a Net Buyer

Average online purchase	£102 – £118
Percentages of repeat customers	26% – 33%
Average income of an Internet shopper	£46,000 – £50,000

Source: Binary Compass Enterprises

b). Global Electronic Commerce Sales Volume

Year	1995	2000	2005
High Estimate	$500 m (£312.50 m)	$32 b (£20 b)	$186 b (£116.25 b)
Low Estimate	$500 m (£312.50 m)	$7 b (£4.3 b)	$76 b (£47.50 b)

Source: Jupiter Communications, SIMBA, Forrester, Visa International

c). The Top Ten Search Terms Entered on All Search Engines:

1. sex

2. nude

3. pictures

4. jpg (J-PEG is a format for online photos)

5. software

6. windows

7. adult

8. women

9. naked

10. erotic.

Source: Webonomics 1998

APPENDIX 6

Country	Ave. Subs. Costs (£)	Subscribers ('000)	Ave. Time Online per month (hrs)
UK	15.42	2,019	11
Germany	14.63	4,557	15
Netherlands	14.04	884	15
France	9.01	982	9
Spain	6.64	397	11
Norway	5.61	334	19
Sweden	3.21	924	13

Source: Datamonitor 1999

APPENDIX 7: USEFUL WEB SITES FOR SMALL BUSINESSES

www.britishchambers.org.uk

The UK Chambers of Commerce Web site includes advice on all aspects of business especially for prospective exporters.

www.businesseurope.com

Business Europe provides information on trade fairs, a bulletin board and additional information from a wide range of sources.

www.businesslead.com

Offers guides, tips, ideas and advice for small businesses.

www.businesslink.co.uk

The Web site for England's network of advice centres for business.

www.cableol.net/grosvenor/cobcoe

The Council of British Chambers of Commerce in Continental Europe's Web site.

www.cbi.org.uk

The Web site for the Confederation of British Industry. The CBI is the UK's leading employers' organisation.

www.ces.eu.int/en/acs/fr_acs_default.htm

English version Web site of the European Economic and Social Committee (ESC).

www.companieshouse.gov.uk

Companies' House provide all relevant information on company registration and the facility of UK company searches.

www.cor.eu.int

The EU's Committee of the Regions Web site provides topical and regional updates and information regarding grants and funding.

www.dpr.gov.uk

Offers information regarding data protection and data about users registered with the Office of the Data Protection Registrar.

www.dti.gov.uk/public/frame6.html

This Department of Trade and Industry Web page concentrates on topics regarding export and investment.

www.enterprise-ireland.com

Enterprise Ireland brings together the key marketing, technology, business development and training initiatives through which the Government of Ireland supports the growth of Irish industry.

www.epo.co.at/epo

Information about the European Patent Office, registration procedures and a searchable database of patent attorneys across Europe.

www.euen.co.uk

A EU Employers Network forum and support is specifically for employers across Europe, with information on topics such as employer participation.

www.europages.com

Europages is a large directory of companies across Europe, searchable by name, product and service. There's also business news, a guide to Europe and a diary of international trade fairs.

www.fsb.org.uk

The Federation of Small Businesses (FSB) provide information specific to small businesses; from law changes to virus warnings.

www.hmce.gov.uk

The HM Customs and Excise's Web site is full of advice on VAT and custom's regulations.

www.iab.net

The Internet Advertising Bureau use this site to help promote and maximise the use and effectiveness of advertising on the Internet.

www.iccwbo.org

The International Chamber of Commerce is the world business organisation that represents enterprises of all sizes and all sectors of the world.

www.inlandrevenue.gov.uk

This site provides information on income tax, national insurance contributions, corporation tax, capital gains tax etc. It has a particularly useful page regarding self-assessment.

www.internic.co.uk

The UK's International NIC direct online domain name registration service.

www.iol.ie/sfa/

The Small Firms Association is an organisation which represents and supports small business in Ireland.

www.ispo.cec.be

ISPO was conceived to act as a broker between parties who want to work together on IT projects. This site contains information on the organisation.

www.regionlink.com

A site for information about business throughout Europe, aiming to promote smaller enterprises via the Internet.

www.tec.co.uk

This Training & Enterprise Council's site provides news, a discussion forum, links and learning resources for small business.

www.yahoo.co.uk/Business_and_Economy

This page lists business links to most subjects and sectors relevant to any small firm.

APPENDIX 8

The Top Ten Items Most Purchased Over the Internet:

1. Personal Travel

2. Computer Software

3. Event Tickets

4. Banking

5. Business Travel

6. Computer Hardware

7. Music

8. Food

9. Books

10. Vacations.

Source: www.pegasusri.com/marketsize.htm. August, 1999

GLOSSARY

Access Provider

The company (also called an Internet service provider or ISP) that sells access and provides the method of connecting customers to the Internet.

alt.binaries

The grouping of Usenet conferences, alt. binaries ranges from the fairly innocuous alt.binaries.autographs to altogether more sinister pornographic content. The files found on these conferences varies from illegal copies of software to scanned pornography.

AltaVista

Digital's powerful search engine. This engine searches through more than 30 million pages found on 275,600 servers, and 4 million articles from 14,000 Usenet news groups. AltaVista is accessed more than 17 million times per week day.

AOL

America Online. One of the biggest Internet service providers in the world.

Application

A computer program such as a word processor or spreadsheet.

Applet

An applet is a Java (www.sun.com) or ActiveX (www.microsoft.com) program designed to run in a Web browser and implement features (particularly interactive features) on a Web page.

Archie

Provides a method of searching for publicly available files on the Internet.

Arpanet

The Advanced Research Projects Agency (ARPA) of the US Department of Defence was set up in the early 70s. This network and its structure became the model for the Internet.

Backbones

The central network infrastructure of the Internet is often referred to as the "backbone" and it is this that allows data to travel from one network to another. Many Internet access providers in the EU use the backbones of other larger providers to carry data most offer their backbone access to third-party access providers.

Bandwidth

This is used to explain how much data can be sent through a connection to the Net. Typically text files use little bandwidth while pictures and sound much more. This digital traffic is measured in bits per second, so a modem running at 57,600bps is twice as fast as one at 28,800bps. The term has been stolen from electronics, where bandwidth is used to measure in kilohertz (KHz) or megahertz (MHz) the frequency at which analogue devices carry electronic signals.

Baud Rate

The speed of a modem measured in *bits* per second.

Berners-Lee, Tim

This is the man who invented the World Wide Web. An Oxford University graduate, Berners-Lee was an engineer at CERN, the European Particle Physics Laboratory in Geneva. Back in 1989, he proposed a global hypertext project, to be known as the World Wide Web. The first World Wide Web server and the first client were written by Berners-Lee for the NeXT computer. In 1994, he joined the Laboratory for Computer Science as director of the W3 Consortium. www.w3.org/pub/WWW/People/Berners-Lee/.

BIOS

Basic Input Output System. A set of routines used to handle basic input/output.

Bit

The smallest unit of measurement for computer data.

Bitmap

A set of bits that represent an graphic image.

Bookmark

A stored web site or web page URL that can be accessed at the click of a mouse from the Bookmarks menu of a browser.

Bps

Bits per second. The speed by which modems are rated.

Bridges

Computer which provides a connection for other computers within a local area so that can work together and share information.

Browser

A software application that allows browsing of the Internet for information.

Bus

In computing, a bus is a computer system along which the data is transmitted back and forth.

Byte

The smallest possible unit of data storage. The size of a computer file is referred to in bytes.

Cable

Cable is predicted to solve bandwidth problems. Cable and cable modems are soon to be incorporated into Internet connectivity.

Cache

A temporary storage space where your Web browser stores the files downloaded from the Internet to speed up your Web browsing.

Case Sensitive

Some computer programs and languages do not distinguish between upper and lower case characters. However, the Internet does.

CGI

Common Graphics Interface — the ISO/IEC 9636 standard, Interfacing Techniques for Dialogues with Graphical Devices. A device-independent interface standard between a graphical input or output device and a graphics utility program. CGI is similar to a "compiler" that converts most computer languages (but mostly PERL) into a format usable to your web pages.

Client

Software that requests data from a server (such as *newsreader*, *Web browser*, or FTP program).

Cookies

Some web sites place a "cookie" on your computer when you visit it. This is done so that if you return to the site, it will be able to read the cookie to see what you did last visit and add more information.

Cyberspace

A term meaning the entire world of computers linked together.

Database

A PC filing cabinet for data with some powerful searching capabilities.

Dialogue Box

A window, which pops up to give you information, or requires you to input information.

Dial-up

The act of (temporarily) using telephone lines or ISDN networks to connect computers to the Internet.

DNS

Domain Name System. The system that regulates the naming of computers on the Internet.

Domain Names

Without domain names users would have to type in IP numbers to connect to other computers on the Internet. Domain names are the names given to a collection of machines at a particular site. The domain name forms the latter part of a URL (e.g. sony.com in the URL http://www.sony.com). It is also used in email addresses (e.g. name@sony.com).

Download

The act of taking information or applications from the World Wide Web and storing it on a computer's hard disk.

EDI

Electronic Data Interchange. Used by businesses to maintain JIT (Just-In-Time) stock levels.

EFTS

Electronic Funds Transfer System. Generally, the use of computers in effecting payments between individuals and/or organisations. In some cases the term is used to refer to advanced future systems in which debits and credits are made simultaneously with the transactions that give rise to them. In other cases its use covers all computer-based funds transfer systems, including: ATM (automated teller machines), EFT-POS and debit cards, EFT-EDI (electronic data interchange) systems and the US automated clearing house (ACH) network. There are several major world-wide EFT networks, including the SWIFT (Society for World-Wide Interbank Financial Transmission) network.

E-mail

Short for electronic mail: a means of sending and receiving messages via the Internet.

E-mail Address

The unique address which allows people to send mail.

Emoticons

Combination of punctuation marks frequently used in emails to indicate the tone of voice. ☺ for example indicates happiness or approval.

Encryption

A method of coding data to prevent unauthorised access, most commonly used on the Net to protect e-mail or credit card transactions.

FAQ

Frequently asked questions. An FAQ file is a compilation of questions and answers stored on the Internet that helps newcomers to the Web.

Firewalls

Basically a piece of hardware or software that sits between a Web server and the rest of a corporate network so that those who log onto the server cannot get onto a company's network.

File

Any piece of data stored on your computer; e.g. a program or a document.

Flame

To abuse an Internet user publicly by e-mail.

Frame Relay

A form of network transmission in which packets from different lower-speed sources are encapsulated together to form a very large frame, up to several hundred bytes in length, which is then transported as a unit on a single higher-speed bearer. The frame will usually have a fixed length, and more or less fixed internal structure. The fixed size and relatively simple internal structure of the frames means that the switching activity can be implemented with a considerable degree of hardware assistance, while the larger frame size reduces the ratio of overheads to useful payload. In particular it is possible to allow packets to enter or leave the frame relay system using an assembly of standardised products.

FTP

File Transfer Protocol is a technology that allows data to be trans-ferred across the Net. Although most browsers include FTP sup-port the best option is for a company to equip itself with an FTP program such as Cute FTP from www.cuteftp.com.

Gb

A thousand megabytes. A measurement of storage space of a hard disk.

GIF

Graphic Interchange Format. The most common format for com-pressed graphics on the Internet.

Gopher

Gopher is essential for anyone looking up information on the Internet. Gopher does the hard work and categorises the information itself so the user does not have to worry about where it is stored.

Graphics Card

The part of a PC that controls the screen's image. Most PCs are fitted with 2D cards as standard – which is all that Windows 95 needs – but many new games require a 3D graphics card as well.

Hacking

Gaining unauthorised access to a computer.

Hard Drive (or Hard Disk)

A high-capacity storage device that a PC uses for programs and data, measured in gigabytes. Information held on a hard disk is safe when the power is withdrawn.

Hardware

The computer and all its physical peripherals e.g. monitor, keyboard, printer etc.

Homepage

The opening page of a web site.

Host

A computer on the Internet that allows users to connect to it.

Host Name

The name given to the host computer.

HTML

A derivative of the Standard Graphical Mark Up Language (SGML), HyperText Markup Language (HTML) is the language used to create Web pages. The simple text formatting and linking commands can be created in a text editor although programs such as *HTML Pro* from SoftQuad, *Pagemill* from Adobe and *Internet Assistant* for Word from Microsoft make the whole thing simple. Resources online include the Ultimate HTML Resource at www.lookup.com/Homepages/69499/home.html

HTTP

Hyper Text Transfer Protocol. The normal way of transferring HTML documents between servers and browsers.

Hypertext

Mainly used on web pages, clicking on this text will open a link to another web page. It is in a different colour to the body text and often underlined to make it stand out.

Hypertext Link

A key feature of the Web is that HTML allows documents anywhere on the Web (see Link).

Hubs

Computers which tie other computers together to allow them to combine their memory and work together to process information beyond their individual capacity.

Internet (or Net)

An international network that links thousands of computers, using telephone and cable links.

IRC

Internet Relay Chat (IRC); live discussions on the Internet. Divided into servers and channels where conversations take place in real-time. Users can download an application such as mIRC from www.geocities.com/SiliconValley/Park/6000/index.html.

IP

Internet Protocol allows data to be stored in packets that can be sent across multiple networks to an address, which is usually in the form of an IP number. Each individual computer on the Internet has an IP number and dial-up customers are dynamically given IP addresses every time they log on; allowing them to behave as if they were permanently connected to the network.

IP Address

The unique numeric address of a computer on the Internet.

ISDN

ISDN is the next stage up from modem connections and is a network connection technology that offers a considerable increase in speed. A special adapter is required for a computer although the costs of calls are similar to the cost of normal phone calls.

ISP

Internet Service Provider. An organisation from which access to the Internet can be bought. AOL, MSN, and CompuServe are some of the biggest names in the EU.

Java

Perhaps the most significant Internet technology of recent years, Java was developed by Sun (www.sun.com). Java is a programming language that allows tiny programs, or applets, to be created and sent over the network. Initially much Java development led to nice animations and games but more compelling uses are now starting to appear.

JPEG (or JPG)

A bitmap file format for compressing images on the internet.

56Kbps

The speed at which a modem will run. 56Kbps is the current top-speed modem available. The faster the speed, the quicker you will be able to download web pages etc.

Leased Line

A permanently open telephone line connecting a computer to the Internet.

Logging On

Entering user details to access the Internet.

Link

An instant electronic gateway from one Web site to another, or to different pages within the same site.

Mailbox

An address at which e-mail is received.

Mb Megabyte

A unit of computer information.

Meta Tags

These are HTML tags that surround keywords and phrases when submitting a site to a search engine.

MHz (Megahertz)

A unit of measurement of frequency. 1 megahertz = 1,000,000 hertz.

Microsoft Internet Explorer (IE)

Internet browser. Has recently taken over as the most used browser in the UK.

Midi

Musical Instrument Digital Interface. A special interface that lets your computer control musical instruments, such as a keyboard or drum machine. To create a MIDI set-up you need a MIDI interface for your PC, which is often part of a sound card, and a cable that runs to your musical instrument.

Modem

A device that connects two computers via a telephone line.

Mosaic

One of the most common browser programs.

Motherboard

The main printed circuit board inside your computer.

Mouse

This device controls the movement of the cursor on the computer screen.

MP3

MPEG Layer 3. A way of highly compressing digital sound so that it takes less time to download and uses less hard disk space. CD audio, for example, can be compressed by a factor of 10.

MPEG

The standard for compressing audio and video files over the Internet.

MSN

Microsoft's online service was launched in August 1995 as a proprietary system that used the company's own development tools. Later Microsoft turned MSN into a Web-based Internet service.

Netiquette

Good behaviour on the Internet.

Netscape Navigator

Internet browser. It can be downloaded for a free trial from Netscape's site. (www.netscape.com)

Network Computer

Based on Oracle's standard for low-cost Internet-ready devices, The Network Computer will be a low-cost machine that connects to a TV or monitor. Local storage will be kept to a minimum as applications, such as Java, will deliver all the applications needed via the Net.

Newsgroup

Name given to an electronic bulletin board on the Internet.

Online Service Providers

Online Services Providers (OSPs) provide access to the Internet, often through a local POP. They are known as OSPs to distinguish them from the smaller ISPs. Connecting to the Internet through an OSP is an alternative to regional or local ISPs. These online companies are commercial concerns that have their own databases and information services for their own subscribers to access in addition to getting onto the Internet. There are three global online services providing Internet access: AOL (America On-Line), CompuServe and MSN (Microsoft Network). The term OSP is falling into disuse as most large ISPs now provide content etc.

Packet

This is a unit of data, which is typically part of a file, prepared for transport across a network.

Pentium II & III

Improved versions of Intel's original Pentium processor, which powers millions of PCs around the world.

Ping

Ping is a network command and application that allows a user to probe networked computers to see if they are connected and on-line.

Plug-ins

An additional piece of software that is sometimes required to enjoy the full facility of a web site, such as the display of video clips.

Point of Presence (PoP)

Areas where a user can dial in to their account without placing a long-distance call.

POP3

Post Office Protocol Number 3 (POP3). Not a "point of presence" (POP) but a method of sending email messages.

Point-to-Point Protocol (PPP)

The rules that enable a dial-up connection to connect to a host computer.

Portal

A web site that provides all the services people are likely to use online.

Post Office Protocol (POP)

A protocol that manages Internet mail until picked up at an ISP.

Processor

Also known as the central processing unit or CPU, the processor is the heart of the computer. It does most of the hard work and the faster the processor, the better the system is likely to be.

PSTN

Public Switched Telephone Network.

QuickTime

Apple's movie technology, QuickTime, allows you to play audio and video clips and is now built into Navigator. QuickTime VR is impressive and creates 3D worlds that can be rotated and moved through. For examples try http://qtvr.quicktime.apple.com/. For any of the QuickTime family of software go to http://quicktime. apple.com.

RSA

Public/private-key encryption standard. The encryption algo-rithm commonly used on the Internet and incorporated within the secure sockets layer (SSL) is RSA, a public/private-key encryption standard, which is based on the problem of factoring large numbers. The larger the number, the longer it takes to compute its factors, and this is the basis of RSA's security. It has now been shown however, it is theoretically possible to break RSA without having to solve the underlying factoring problem.

Router

A device that transfer data between one or more networks.

SCSI

Stands for Small Computer Systems Interface. A high-speed parallel interface sometimes used to connect PCs to peripheral devices such as disk drives and scanners.

Search Engine

A web site dedicated to helping to find information simply by typing words or phrases into a search text box.

Server

The central computer making services and data available.

Shareware

Software that can be downloaded from the Internet for a free trial period, or totally free of charge. (The latter is commonly known as *Freeware*).

Shareware.com

The Internet is full of free software and www.shareware.com is the place to find it. This huge site categorises thousands of applications and allows a search for elusive software.

Shockwave

Macromedia produce Shockwave which allows designers to incorporate Director movies and animations into Web pages. www.macromedia.com.

Sig Files

Signature files are details a user put at the end of mail messages. They usually include a user's name and contact information but often include a favourite quote or examples of ASCIIart. http://grid.let.rug.nl/~welling/sigs.html.

Smart Card

Invented in 1974, a smart card is a payment system that allows the user to "load" electronic currency or credit on to a card and send it at merchants with the necessary reading systems installed.

SMDS

Switched Multimegabit Data Service. A switched broadband service that is being introduced by a number of public network operators (PNO). The intention is that SMDS will support data services at a range of bit rates from 1.536 Mbps (2.048 Mbps in Europe) up to 45 Mbps (34 Mbps in Europe) and subsequently at higher speeds, certainly as high as 155 Mbps. SMDS is a connectionless system, based on variable-length packets with a payload of up to 9188 bytes. Each packet contains both the source and destination addresses, the addresses being the same as ISDN addresses and globally unique.

Spam

In the Internet world spamming is posting a message (usually uninvited) to a number of users or newsgroups, usually of a commercial nature. There are services which claim they can get you taken off spammers lists. http://drsvcs.com/nospam/.

Strouds Apps List

Stroud is the home of a collection of Internet utilities and applications and a good place to find links to all the latest software. The site also has reviews of most of the packages and is updated daily at www.cwsapps.com.

T-1 and T-3

Special high-speed and heavy-traffic lines which connect networks to the Internet backbones through router computers.

TCP

Transmission Control Protocol is a reliable connection-orientated protocol that allows a byte stream originating on one machine to be delivered without error on any other machine on the Internet. It fragments the incoming byte stream into discrete messages and passes each one onto the Internet layer. At the destination, the receiving TCP process resembles the received messages into the output stream. TCP also handles flow control to make sure a fast sender cannot swamp a slow receiver with more messages than it can handle.

TCP/IP

Transmission Control Protocol/Internet Protocol is the set of rules that allows computers to communicate over the Internet. Every computer connected to the Internet needs a copy. When data such as an email or a Web page is sent or received, it is divided into tiny segments called packets. Each packet has the sender's Internet address and the receiver's address. The first layer, TCP, allows computers to establish a connection and exchange data. Internet Protocol is the postal system that recognises the address of each packet.

Telnet

Telnet allows a user to connect directly to another computer that has a Telnet server. This includes services such as the CIX bulletin board and CompuServe.

Upload

To transfer information from one computer to another directly over the Internet.

Upgrade

To make an improvement to your current system; usually changing old software or hardware for up-to-date versions.

URL

The Universal Resource Locator is the command that points to the Web address. This facility means users do not have to remember lengthy and unmemorable IP addresses.

UNIX

UNIX is at the centre of the Internet. UNIX is the great academic, networking operating system and is still popular as a Web server.

USB

The universal serial bus is a recent standard for connecting peripherals, such as scanners and printers, to PCs quickly and simply.

Usenet

Usenet is a series of discussion forums mirrored on servers around the world. A user subscribes to a group they are interested in and joins in the discussion. There are more than 16,000 newsgroups. Demon Internet, which has one of the biggest news servers in the country, handles 2Gb of news per day. If a user's provider does not carry newsgroups there are public servers. www.geocities.com/Hollywood/2513/news.html.

VGA

Video Graphics Array. A video adaptor for displaying with a resolution of 640 x 480 pixels in up to 256 colours.

Virus

A program designed to cause problems that can be transmitted from computer to computer.

VRML

Developed by Mark Pesce, VRML is a standard that allows web sites to be replaced with 3D rotational shapes and spaces. Netscape includes Live 3D VRML support in the latest version of Navigator. For a list of top VRML sites visit www.virtus.com/vrmlsite.html.www.sdsc.edu/vrml/.

Wav File (.wav)

Windows' audio file format used for saving and loading sounds to and from disc.

Web Hosting

The act of publishing a web site.

Web Site

A collection of documents or information published on the World Wide Web.

WWW

World Wide Web. A system based on HyperText that links information and files on different computer around the Internet. The World Wide Web tends to represent the commercial part of the Internet.

Yahoo!

Yahoo! is an essential Web site. The premise is simple; by breaking the Web down into a number of categories and sub-categories Yahoo! acts as a giant directory to thousands of sites. www.yahoo.com.

BIBLIOGRAPHY

Publications

Anderton, A. *Economics* (Causeway Press Ltd.,: UK) 1992

Beynon-Davies, P. *Information Systems Development* (Macmillan: London) 1989

Brown, A.J. *Introduction to the World Economy,* 2nd ed. (Unwin University Books: London) 1994

Business Exchange & Mart, 24 September, 1998

BYTE (McGraw-Hall Co. Inc.: USA) February, 1994

BYTE (McGraw-Hall Co. Inc.: USA) January-December 1997

BYTE (McGraw-Hall Co. Inc.: USA) January-February 1998

Campaign Magazine, 22 May, 1998

Capron, H.L. *Systems Analysis and Design* (The Benjamin / Cummings Publishing Company, Inc.: USA) 1986

Computing, 10 September, 1998

Computing, 17 September, 1998

Computing, 8 October, 1998

Computing, 6 November, 1998

Computing, 19 November, 1998

Computing, 8 April, 1999

Computing, 22 April, 1999

Computer Act!ve Magazine (VNU Business Publications: UK), 13 August, 1998

Computer Act!ve Magazine, 27 August, 1998

Computer Bulletin, September, 1998

Computer Dictionary (Microsoft Press: USA) 1991

"Creating a Favourable Business Environment for Electronic Commerce: The European Approach." http://europe.eu.int/comm/dg03/speeches/sm980225.htm

Curtis, G. *Business Information Systems* 2nd ed. (Addison Wesley) 1995

Dawes, B., *International Business: A European Perspective* (Stanley Thornes [Publishers] Ltd.: London) 1995

Dibb, D. Lyndon, S. Williams, M.P. & Ferrell, O.C. *Markeing: Concepts and Strategies* (Hought Miffin Co.: London) 1991

Deaton, A. & Muellbauer, J. *Economics and Consumer Behaviour* (London: Cambridge University Press) 1980

Ehrenberg, A.S.C. & Pyatt, F.G. *Consumer Behaviour* (London: Penguin Books) 1969

Encyclopaedia of Computer Science, 3rd ed. (Clapman & Hall: London) 1993

Financial Mail on Sunday, 12 July 1998

Financial Mail on Sunday, 2 August, 1998

Financial Mail on Sunday, 9 August, 1998

Financial Mail on Sunday, 16 August, 1998

Financial Mail on Sunday, 30 August, 1998

Financial Mail on Sunday, 20 September, 1998

Financial Mail on Sunday, 11 October, 1998

Financial Mail on Sunday, 28 February, 1999

Foxall, G. *Consumer Choice* (Macmillan: London) 1983

Foxall, G. *Consumer Psychology in Behavioural Perspective* (Routledge: London) 1990

Frost, A. & Norris, M. Exploiting the Internet: Understanding and Exploiting an Investment in the Internet (John Wiley & Sons: UK) 1997

Gates, W. *PC Advisor Magazine*, February, 1998

Greenly, G.E. *Strategic Management* (Prentice-Hall: London) 1989

Heathcote, P.M. *Tackling Computer Projects* (Guernsey Press Co: Guernsey) 1992

Hodges, M.E. & Sasnett, R.M. *Multimedia Computing* (Addison-Wesley: UK) 1992

International Journal of Project Management Vol. 8 No. 4 Nov. 1990 (Butterworth-Heinemann Ltd: UK)

International Journal of Project Management Vol. 11 No. 4 Nov. 1990 (Butterworth-Heinemann Ltd: UK)

Internet Business Magazine, Issue 18, July, 1998

Internet Magazine (Emap Apex Publications Ltd.), April, 1998

Internet Magazine (Cradely Print: UK), July, 1998

Internet Works Magazine, July, Issue 7, 1998, p. 10

Internet Works Magazine, Summer 98, Issue 8, 1998

Internet Works Magazine, Issue 9, August, 1998

it@mailonsunday.co.uk

Jamsa, K. *Instant Multimedia* (John Wigley & Sons, Inc.: USA) 1993

Jeffcoate, J. *Multimedia in Practice* (Prentice Hall: London) 1995

Johnson, G. & Scholes, K. *Exploring Corporate Strategy: Text and Cases*, 3rd ed. Prentice Hall Europe: London. 1993

Jones, J.P. *What's in a Name? Advertising and the Concept of Brands* (Gower Publishing: UK) 1986

Joyce, T. *How Advertising Works* (London: Walter Thompson) 1974

Kalakota, Ravi & Whinston, Andrew B. *Electronic Commerce — A Manager's Guide*. (London: Addison-Wesley) 1997

Keflas, A.G., *Global Business Strategy: A Systems Approach* (South-West Publishing Co.: USA) 1990

Layzell, P. & Loucopoulo, S. *Systems Analysis and Development* (Chartwell-Bratt: Sweden) 1989

Lewis, P. *Information Systems Development* (Pitman Publishing: UK) 1994

Lowndes, D. *Marketing*: *The Use of Advertising* (Pergamon Press Ltd.: London) 1969

Maber, J., W3Launch - *Secure Software Menus on the World*, http://www.leeds.ac.uk/bionet/w3launch/w3l-home.htm

Marketing Magazine, 29 May, 1998

Mittra, S.S. *Structured Techniques of Systems Analysis, Design and Implementation* (John Wigley & Sons: USA) 1988

Mowen, J.C. *Consumer Behaviour* (Prentice-Hall International Ltd. (UK): London) 1995

Murphy, J.M. *Branding: A Key Marketing Tool* (Chairman, Interbrand/Novamark Group: London) 1987

Multimedia (Dorling Kindersley: London) 1996

Negroponte, Nicholas (1996): *Being Digital*. Random House. Parts of the book are available at http://www.obs-us.com:80/obs/english/books/nn/bdintro.htm

Network News, 9 September, 1998

Network News, 30 September, 1998

OECD: Dismantling the Barriers to Global Electronic Commerce. http://www.oecd.org/sti/it/ec/prod/dismantl.htm

Pascoe, E. *Internet: The Cyberian Connection* (Purple Training Ltd: London) 1994

PC Advisor Magazine, February, 1998

PC Direct Magazine (Zif-Davis Ltd: UK) March, 1998

PC KnowHow Magazine, Part 4 (ET Heron & Co.: London) 1998

PC Guide Magazine, August, 1998

PC Weekly, 24 October, 1998

PC Weekly, 26 January, 1999

Pocket Strategy, The Economist Books (Profile Books Ltd: London) 1998

Power, Cheney & Crow. *Structured Systems Development* (Prentice-Hall: London) 1989

Riley, F, *Understanding IT: A Review of Hypermedia Authoring Packages* (USDU: Sheffield) 1994

Roche, B. (Minister for Small Business) *Financial Mail on Sunday*, 12 July, 1998

Runyon, K.E. *Consumer Behaviour* (London: Charles E. Merrill Publishing Co.) 1980

Schneier, B. *E-Mail Security* (John Wiley & Sons Inc.: UK) 1995

Size Analysis of United Kingdom Businesses (PA1003A) (The Stationery Office: UK) 1997

Sommerville, I. *Software Engineering* 4th ed. (Addison-Wesley Publishing Co: UK) 1992

Shapiro, J. *Collaborative Computing: Multimedia Across the Network* (Academic Press Ltd.: UK) 1996

Skinner, B.F. *The Behaviour of Organisms* (Appleton-Century: New York) 1938

Statistical Press Release, Small and Medium Enterprise (SME) Statistics for the UK, P/97/459, Department of Trade and Industry (Stationery Office: UK) July 1997

Sunday Times, *Getting Wired: Computing for Small and Medium-Sized Firms*, 19 October 1997

Sunday Times (Sounding Off), 5 July, 1998

Sunday Times (Money), 30 August, 1998

Sunday Times (Innovation), 6 September, 1998

T3 (Future Publishing: London) February, 1998

Taoka, G.M. & Beeman, D.R., *International Business: Environments, Institutions and Operations* (Harper Collins Publishers Ltd.) 1991

Tanenbaum, A.S., *Computer Networks* 3rd ed. (Prentice Hall International Ltd.: London) 1996

Tuck, M. *How Do We Choose?* (Methuen & Co. Ltd.: London) 1976

Visa International: *SET Specification*, http://www.visa.com/cgi-bin/vee/nt/ecomm/set/intro.html?2+0

Wall, L. and Schwartz, R.L., *Programming Perl* (O'Reilly & Associates, Inc.: USA) 1991

What PC? Magazine (VNU Publications: London), June, 1998

Woods, W.A. *Consumer Behaviour* (North Holland: New York) 1981

Zimmerman, P. et al. *Pretty Good Privacy: Public Key Encryption for the Masses,* ftp://unix.hensa.ac.uk/pub/uunet/security/virus/crypt/pgp July 1993

Websites

http://connexion.parallax.com/seduct/

http://europe.eu.int/comm/dg03/speeches/sm980225.htm

http://faxsav.com/faxsavinternet

http://ntxc.com

http://sky-l.com

www.abc.com

www.abtanet.com

www.actinic.co.uk

www.addme.com

www.adobe.co.uk

www.adultcheck.com

www.afd.co.uk

www.altavista.com

www.amazon.com

www.barclaysquare.co.uk

www.bargainholidays.com

www.bbc.co.uk

www.bookpages.co.uk

www.bookshop.co.uk

www.british-airways.com

www.btinternet.com

www.btinternet.com/~ne.mas/

www.btinternet.com/~trophysud.htm

www.cnn.com

www.cardcorp.co.uk

www.catapult.co.uk

www.cdnow.com

www.cheapflights.co.uk

www.checkdomain.com

www.commerce.net/news/press

www.conveyancingdirect.co.uk

www.copernic.com

www.cybercash.com/banks/

www.datamonitor.com

www.desktoplawyer.net

www.digicash.com

www.djhgraphics.com

www.domainnames.co.uk

www.dpr.gov.uk

www.dti.gov.uk/export.control

www.easyjet.com

www.eaglestar.co.uk

www.eaglestardirect.co.uk

www.ebid.com

www.elibrary.com

www.enterprisecity.co.uk

www.epoll.com

www.excite.com

www.expedia.co.uk

www.exploit.com

www.faxscape.com

www.finger.com

www.fingering.com

www.fist.com

www.fletch.com.uk

www.flightbookers.com

www.forrester.com

www.freeuk.co.uk

www.ft.com

www.guardian.co.uk

www.gobble.com

www.goto.com

www.heartofengland.co.uk

www.hitbox.com

www.hotbot.com

www.hmce.gov.uk

www.iab.net

www.imusic.com

www.infoseek.com

www.internic.net

www.irc.com

www.isitsafe.com

www.jfax.com

www.kagi.com

www.lastminute.com

www.leisurehunt.com

www.linkexchange.com

www.liszt.com

www.lycos.com

www.mansfield-motors.com

www.mbe.com

www.metacrawler.com

www.motortrader.com

www.msn.com

www.mytaxi.co.uk

www.netbanx.com

www.netbenefit.co.uk

www.netcentric.com

www.netcraft.com/survey/

www.netnames.co.uk

www.nua.com

www.pa.press.net

www.perseus.com

www.phuck.com

www.phuk.co.uk

www.pierce.com

www.plade.com

www.pluckit.com

www.powermalls.com

www.pricejam.co.uk

www.propertymarket.co.uk

www.pub-paraphernalia.com

www.quixell.com

www.reuters.com

www.rsa.com

www.sade.com

www.sj.com

www.samplenet.com

www.screentrade.com

www.searchenginewatch.com

www.shopcreator.com

www.smallbizsearch.com

www.snap.com

www.spank.com

www.standard.co.uk

www.statmarket.com

www.submit.com

www.sykescottages.co.uk

www.teddingtoncheese.co.uk

www.telegraph.co.uk

www.telinco.net

www.the-graphics.co.uk

www.theinternetraffle.com

www.thesuitcase.com

www.the-times.co.uk

www.ticketmaster.co.uk

www.totalweb.co.uk

www.travelocity.com

www.tucows.com

www.ubid.com

www.watkinsbooks.com

www.webcrawler.com

www.webprovider.com

www.webstats.com

www.world-callnet.com

www.yahoo.com

www.zyris.com

INDEX